DANCE
OF DEATH

DANCE
OF DEATH

— THE LIFE OF —
JOHN FAHEY
AMERICAN GUITARIST

STEVE LOWENTHAL

CHICAGO
REVIEW
PRESS
An A Cappella Book

Library of Congress Cataloging-in-Publication Data
Lowenthal, Steve.
  Dance of death : the life of John Fahey, American guitarist / Steve Lowenthal.
      pages cm
  Includes bibliographical references and index.
  ISBN 978-1-61374-519-9
  1. Fahey, John, 1939–2001. 2. Guitarists—United States—Biography. I. Title.

ML419.F35L69 2014
787.87092—dc23
[B]

2014007354

Interior design: PerfecType, Nashville, TN

Printed in the United States of America
5 4 3 2 1

CONTENTS

FOREWORD

I saw John Fahey in performance only once, very late in his journey through American blues, roots, and expressive mystery—in the late 1990s, only a few years before his death, at a New York club, Tramps. It was a telling measure of the guitarist's cult heroism and odyssey of troubles to that point: the room was packed with older fans, recent devotees, and alternative-rock cachet—I stood against a wall near the low, small stage with Sonic Youth guitarist Thurston Moore and Fahey's great critic-champion in that decade, Byron Coley. But that night, Fahey was an opening act, warming up the room for another dogged, gifted folk-blues survivor, John Hammond Jr. History was in the house, in abundance. Fortune determined the billing.

Fahey's set was a rare local sighting. It also came with baggage and warning. Fahey's poetic facility and improvisational brio—the soul and dazzle of his routinely breathtaking 1960s recordings—had suffered through neglect, ill health, poverty, and his long, perverse war with celebrity and public admiration. And Fahey—who infused the acoustic guitar with a pioneering, orchestral luminescence and story-telling articulation on (to name just a handful of diamonds) 1965's *The Transfiguration of Blind Joe Death*, 1968's *The Yellow Princess*, and the '68 Christmas present *The New Possiblity*—was playing a Stratocaster, casting rippled shadows of digital delay across his recent electric minimalism, bossa nova sway, and suite-like wandering.

The effect was at once discomfiting and hypnotizing, a quietly
insistent contradiction of Fahey's history and legend, bound up in
a music that felt like he was talking to himself in a crush of strangers. I watched and listened with keen, grateful acceptance, privileged
to be so close to a figure of such revolutionary passion and fusion. I
also knew that Fahey's storied virtuosity—his unprecedented advance
in the 1960s through pioneer folk, Delta blues, and advanced classical harmonies, with complex fingerpicking grace and velocity, to an
invention he wryly dubbed "American Primitive Guitar"—was not
coming back again.

The music he played at Tramps was, nevertheless, classic Fahey:
aggressive in its striving, beautiful in its deep hurt and candor. There
were outbursts over misfiring gear and odd, digressive banter. There
was consistency too. Fahey's lifelong evasion of convention and expectation, on his most eccentric and sublime albums, was just as true
that night, in his playing, manner, and, after the last note, vanishing. I never saw Fahey in his generally acknowledged prime. But I
witnessed the impulse, challenge, and restless artistry at their purest,
just in time.

I would have liked more, earlier. Fahey never made it easy. In
1970—a little over a decade into his recording career, right as I was
discovering the strange, colorful lore and intimate force of his 1968
album *The Voice of the Turtle* in the library at my campus radio station, Fahey already sounded like a magus at a crossroads—itching for
a fight, lost in his work, desperate for peace—in the opening line of
his first *Rolling Stone* article: "I just want to make a whole bunch of
money so I can pay my psychiatric bills." Even in the best of times,

Fahey toured irregularly, elevating and taunting his audiences in equal measure, with a peculiar sense of geography and occasion.

Fahey's descent, by the early 1990s, into itinerant destitution—a compound product of alcoholism, failed relationships, and the Epstein-Barr virus, which struck the energy and precision of his playing to a severe, permanent degree—ironically mirrored the lives of those prewar blues and country singers and specters that Fahey studied and loved on the way to his own records and a UCLA master's degree in folklore and mythology. But Fahey had cultivated anonymity from the start. Half of the original pressing of his self-released 1959 debut, *John Fahey / Blind Joe Death*, was credited to a pseudonymous bluesman, a mask Fahey often used later for both retreat and fun. After Fahey's death in 2001, his friend and collaborator Barry Hansen—a.k.a. Dr. Demento—pointed out to me that three of the tracks on *The Voice of the Turtle*, my entrance into Fahey's music, were old blues 78s that Fahey dubbed from the shellac and credited on the album to Blind Joe Death. To Fahey, that wasn't deceit; it was a prankster's homage.

Fahey was no Delta ghost; he grew up in Takoma Park, Maryland, in a troubled household, under emotional-combat conditions. He was an enterprising loner. Fahey started his own label, Takoma, named after the old neighborhood, to release *John Fahey / Blind Joe Death* and sold copies at the Maryland gas station where he worked, between filling cars. He also slipped copies of the album into local thrift and record stores, making it seem as if the LP had arrived by vapor, under cover of darkness—a prophetic gesture for a man who made most of his music away from the mainstream industry, slipping in and out of earshot, always in some kind of motion or flight. Even as he entered the world, with that first album, Fahey was expert in the guile of exile.

Steve Lowenthal has written the first major historical and critical biography of John Fahey. It is a vivid, rigorously reported examination of his life, the emotional and creative birth of his genius, and its rich, magnificent, and often confounding legacy on record and in performance. There are memories from those he loved, tested, crossed, and in some cases abandoned. It is a book with a ready-made, still-expanding soundtrack: in 2011, the archival imprint Dust-to-Digital added to the more than forty original studio and live albums in Fahey's discography, compiling his primal beginnings—a wild mass of early 78s, demos, and private recordings—in a deluxe five-CD bounty, *Your Past Comes Back to Haunt You: The Fonotone Years 1958–1965*. Fahey loathed nostalgia. He would have adored that title.

Dance of Death is also very much like the music running through this story: thrilling, poignant, cryptic, funny, explosive, harrowing, caring, and fragile—a perfect reflection of the man who made it, at every step in his growth, achievement, anger, and sorrows, right up to the night I saw him at Tramps. Barry Hansen told me something else after Fahey's passing, a story from their trips through the Deep South in the 1960s, seeking the seminal forgotten singers and pickers that made their favorite prewar blues records. "John would buy a lot of 78s," Hansen said. "Some of them were great, some of them he didn't want to keep. So he would throw them out the window as he drove. His favorite thing was to throw these old 78s at bridge abutments and watch them smash." But Hansen added, "He was always careful not to hit anybody."

That was John Fahey in a nutshell. *Dance of Death* is John Fahey in full, at last.

DAVID FRICKE
ROLLING STONE
NOVEMBER 2013

ACKNOWLEDGMENTS

This book would not have been possible without the help of Anthony Pappalardo, Nicholas Katzban, Kris D'Agostino, Erika Storella, Maria Raha, Mike Wolf, Mallory Farrugia, and Yuval Taylor.

Eternal gratitude for the overwhelming support and encouragement over the years of this project from Peter Kolovos, Wayne Rogers, Dominick Fernow, Kate Village, all at VDSQ, Brandon Kavulla, MV Carbon, Paul Gillis, Kevin Bodenheimer, C. Spencer Yeh, Meg Clixby, Michael Bernstein, Chris O'Neal, Kasey Byrne, Angela Sawyer, Paul Familetti, Chris Gray, Beth Lewand, Becka Diamond, Sheila Refael, and Eldad Gothelf, and especially my mother, Sally; my father, Mark; and my sister, Janet.

Special thanks to Laris Kreslins for publishing my first article.

And thanks to Dan Koretsky, Kristen Eshelman at the Thomas J. Dodd Research Center at UConn, Stephen Brower and all at Vanguard, John Allen, Mitch Greenhill, James Jackson Toth, Claudio Guerrieri, Steve Manning, Carlos Giffoni, Marc Minsker, Charles Schmidt, Charles Eppley, Anthony Mangicapra, Matt Krefting, Ted at Feeding Tube Records, the Delta Slider Blog, and the International Fahey Committee / Fahey Files for all their incredible research.

INTRODUCTION

America in the twentieth century was littered with guitar heroes. Most were bombastic, some introspective. Yet among them, John Fahey is perhaps the most mysterious.

Delving into the paradoxical universe of Fahey is often a confusing prospect. Despite his status as a groundbreaking visionary, Fahey's intentions as a man and an artist have remained largely unexamined. He authored and published a memoir in 2001, *How Bluegrass Music Destroyed My Life: Stories by John Fahey*, but as the subtitle suggests, the work is meant to stand as fiction, not a revelation of truth. With so many half truths provided by Fahey in his memoir and liner notes, his story has never been fully told. But by dissecting the myths, more universal truths begin to emerge: those of creative strife and American outsider culture.

The process of telling his story began when I applied to grad school in 2008 with the intention of using an MFA program to launch what would eventually become a full-fledged biography of this mystifying figure in American music. My first step in the research process was to find all the original Fahey LPs and read all of his bizarre and hallucinatory liner notes, which mixed faux academic scholarship and pranks with true references to his life.

One particularly obscure LP was 1965's *The Transfiguration of Blind Joe Death*, which included a thirty-page booklet written by Fahey that same year. In this text, he, as an unnamed omniscient narrator, tells the hallucinatory tale of a student researching his master's thesis on John Fahey. The student finds a shopkeeper and asks, "Did you ever go to any of the clubs around Boston during the 1960s and perchance see or hear of a guitar player named John Fahey? I need any information I can get on him for my Master's thesis. I'm doing it on pre–second foundation artistically creative geniuses." From there, the student is sent to meet a series of Fahey's associates and lovers, a bizarre maze of fantastically surreal characters. The student, who is continually referred to throughout the text as insipid and stupid, eventually finds Fahey trapped in a cave, and becomes trapped himself. While I certainly recognized the strange coincidence here, it became even odder once I realized that the story was set in 2010, and that Fahey had made the protagonist Jewish. I had, quite unwittingly, stepped into a prophesied role, created by John Fahey himself. John predicted that I was coming, and had laid all the traps and mazes for me decades earlier. I took it as a sign I was on the right track.

But that track was far from straight and narrow. Fahey's significance as a musician aside, several other components of his legacy make his story compelling. As a record collector, he opened a door to prewar American music. He discovered and cataloged unknown recordings, such as a 78 of Charley Patton's "Circle Round the Moon," by literally salvaging them from people's trash and dusty basements, reviving music forgotten by history. As a record enthusiast and archivist, he served as a bridge from the past to the present and helped to show how music developed in the recording era.

In his own music, Fahey combined various concepts and approaches. His pastiche of cultural bric-a-brac was deeply postmodern while remaining emotionally relevant. He conveyed a profound sadness at the very core of our shared musical experience, with the blood of the oppressed and dispossessed at its center. Though his is not a story of the blues per se, its language is part of Fahey's vernacular, as are the languages of modern composition, bluegrass—and Maryland.

And Maryland is where the story begins.

WHEN THE CATFISH IS IN BLOOM

"I just watched shades of red pass over everything. This went on for some time. Until the red went away and the black came. The black did come and then it too went away. And so did the memories. It took awhile but the red, the black and the memories all went away. For thirty years they went away and only came out in psychoanalysis."

—John Fahey, *How Bluegrass Music Destroyed My Life*

Takoma Park, Maryland, in the mid-1950s embodied the promise of postwar America at its fullest. Among the first planned commuter suburbs, Takoma Park centered around the B&O Railroad. The Victorian-style houses that dotted the landscape were close enough to Washington, DC, that the employees of the growing government who lived there could get to and from work in a reasonable amount of time, and yet far enough away from the city's unsavory elements that they could feel safe. Deep woods ran through and surrounded the landscape, enough to remind its denizens that it too was once wild. Lush hardwood scenery punctuated the skyline. The Sligo Creek ran through the wilderness, creating a gorgeous naturalism (a nine-mile park ran through the middle of the town). One could easily get lost among the foliage when the light hit and reflected through the multihued leaves of autumn's canopy. Takoma Park was the best of many worlds.

Maryland straddled both sides of the racial and cultural divide, with some areas increasingly liberal and others that hung close to old Southern ideologies. Takoma Park was largely considered among the more left-leaning towns. There still lingered traces of racism, though more generally in the older, more established communities of Montgomery County and nearby Prince George's County. Takoma Park was hardly integrated in the 1950s, with pockets of poverty where poor black or poor white families lived. A public works building close to Ritchie Avenue still had segregated bathrooms. African Americans were employed by the city mainly for trash collection. There were no freeways connecting Takoma Park to other cities, so, as in many suburbs, life remained slow.

The children were the first generation raised in suburban incubation, and they would experience fewer of the hardships of the previous eras, with depressions and world wars behind them. Yet some were left with a hunger for rebellion—or at least for a glimpse into a world that wasn't their own. Unable to connect with the ideas of their time, these teenagers looked backward at the ignored cultural leftovers of years past, finding new value in forms of expression such as blues, bluegrass, and folk music. There were mysteries in records, feelings that were not discussed in any other language. These scratchy, roughly rendered sounds transported listeners back to a time when the problems of 1950s modernity were only distant imaginings.

John Aloysius Fahey was born on February 28, 1939, in Washington, DC, to an adoring mother, Jane Hayes, and a distant father,

Aloysius. Al worked at the National Institutes of Heath and spent a lot of time out of the house. Jane worked as a secretary at the US Geological Survey, though her main focus was her son. In 1944, the Faheys moved from the city to a house on New York Avenue in Takoma Park, an ideal setting for a young family. Al ran the house with strict Catholic discipline. Having grown up in an orphanage, his upbringing had been difficult and filled with abuse, which influenced how he treated his shy, meek son. He controlled his family with a sharp tongue and a firm hand. Both athletic and quick-witted, he quickly grew disappointed in his clumsy son, who rarely showed much interest in sports. Their one common trait was a love of music. Al knew music theory and played Irish harp around the house. With red hair and freckles against his pale skin, his heritage was plain to see. The family often took trips to local fairs to see country and bluegrass performances at places such as the New River Ranch in Rising Sun, Maryland, where they saw artists like the Stanley Brothers perform. In the summer months one could often hear classical music blasting from the open windows of the Fahey house.

Jane was softer than her husband, with the darker features seen in her son. She got by with a pleasant smile, always avoiding difficult subjects and under the thumb of her husband. Jane doted on her child and offered him constant encouragement, becoming his unquestioning champion. "I remember the night we moved into the new house in the suburbs," Fahey recalled in *How Bluegrass Music Destroyed My Life*. "I was sleepy and didn't like what was going on. I remember the following morning, feeling afraid and shy, but preparing myself to go across the street where I saw the local kids hanging out. My mother was encouraging me. She gave me a lot of support."

Those Takoma Park kids formed a neighborhood gang of about fifteen members, mostly boys but a few girls too, and made it a point to know who was moving in, especially the fellow children. Eddie and Larry were two older elementary school kids who decided to admit Fahey, who was about five at the time. The connection to his new neighborhood gang provided him with company and acceptance for the first time. Every day—starting from the day after he met them until sometime in 1948—they came over to his house and took him everywhere they went. "Every day. Everywhere. And they taught me. For some reason they loved me and felt sorry for me, instead of simply snubbing me like most kids would do, they took on the responsibility of rearing me and educating me," recalled Fahey in his memoir, romanticizing his friends' kindness. They raised him in the way only slightly older peers could. They taught him about sex and simplistic politics, and contradicted the ethos of the Catholic Church.

There was a dishonesty in the church that Fahey could never come to terms with. He was taught that the meek inherited the earth, but in school the spoils went to the popular and the strong. Day-to-day normalcies rang false to him. "They made us into monsters," wrote Fahey. "*We* didn't want to be monsters. But we are monsters. And it's all their faults. All they care about is keeping up with the Joneses, whoever in hell the Joneses are."

The competitive nature of navigating social pecking orders left him cold. Fahey instead retreated into a lush fantasy life, along with his friends. Since Takoma Park had brought them all together, they saw the town itself as possessed of magical properties. They dreamed of a secret race of cat people who lived in Magruder Park, one of their favorite local escapes, and only came out at night. The group created its own "history" and pieced together various complex story lines relating to their imagined local demigod, whom they named "the Great Koonaklaster." "Eddie glorified the neighborhood and the people who lived there," remembered Fahey. "He told us all that it was a special place like Valhalla or paradise. The very soil was sacred. The water in the creeks and springs was holy water. The oak trees were the highest in the world. And these oak trees weren't like regular oak trees. They were sacred oak trees planted by the Great Koonaklaster himself while he was creating the world." Through ritualistic chanting the local gang would state their devotion to this imaginary deity in exchange for magical milkshakes and protection from adults. Turtles were considered sacred in their world.

This imaginative spirit helped ameliorate the ever-growing problems at home. In response to his father's temper, Fahey began to take out his frustrations at school. In the seventh grade he was suspended for attacking a female classmate. "But it wasn't fair," wrote Fahey. "After all, I was just doing what my father did to me all the time. Nothing unusual. What was all the fuss about? Oh I knew. I knew. I was wrong and my father was wrong, too. Very much in the wrong. Evil. But I couldn't tell anyone or he might come and get me and kill me."

Things at home soon came to a head. Al and Jane divorced just before John entered high school, and the task of raising their son fell squarely on Jane's shoulders. John and Jane moved out of the house on New York Avenue, where Al would remain for the rest of his life. They moved into Jane's mother's apartment at 7101 New Hampshire Avenue in nearby Prince George's County. Traumatic as divorce would be for any teenager, the split was most likely to John's benefit. Now he no longer had to live with his father, who had nothing kind to say to him or much to offer him. However, Jane struggled to make ends meet, and John never got along with his grandmother, whom he found cold and unloving. The move also separated him from his Takoma Park pals, and he began attending high school in nearby Adelphi.

John developed a hot-headed impulsiveness, overcoming his once-shy demeanor. When he began high school in 1952, the pop charts were filled with bland singers like Rosemary Clooney and Eddie Fisher, everything pleasant and mundane. Fahey began to identify himself as an outsider, feeling he had nothing in common with the popular representations he saw and heard. "I don't know if you boys experienced junior and senior high school the way I did," Fahey said. "I hated them—for various reasons. Aside from the boredom, and the jail-like atmosphere and all the other terrible things, there was no atmosphere for *honesty*." Fahey would soon find a perfect template for his new persona in bad-boy, leather-clad figurehead James Dean. Fahey became a tall young man at six foot four, with a slim yet solid frame. With such an imposing presence, he was able to adopt the role of the rebel easily. And with his black leather jacket and slicked-back hair, he looked ready for trouble—even though he was far from a tough guy.

School seemed to increasingly offend him as he continued into his teens. Neither teachers nor students provided him solace. He began a search for something, anything that he could connect with. If the suburbs were false and couldn't handle the truth, he would look elsewhere for a language to express his disconnection. "They taught us to love each other at the same time they taught us to kill one other," he wrote. "But it wouldn't work with me. It just wouldn't work. I tried. I really tried. But I couldn't make it work. And then I felt guilty. I hated myself. I really did. I hated myself because I couldn't make these two things work together. I couldn't. You don't know how hard I tried to follow those crazy-making instructions, mores, assumptions, actions. Even today, when I think about it, I almost start crying."

Girls he had crushes on, kids who beat him up, and the normal teenage social pressures all seemed liked gigantic, life-altering traumas to him. The everyday trials of growing up from which most recover hit him extremely hard. While many adolescents consider themselves miserable, Fahey seemed more miserable and alienated than most. With his vivid imagination came equally lucid nightmares. "I wanted to kill my parents and then myself," wrote Fahey. "That's what the strange dreams meant. I wanted to kill us because there was something wrong with us. And everyone knew it, too."

He sought refuge in music. One day, while flipping through the radio stations, he became drawn to the instrumental tapestry of classical music. Fahey embraced the strident power of revolutionary Russian composers; they became the first soundtrack to his rebellion. In his memoir he imagined vicious fantasies: "At Mount Rainier Junior High School, in the same town where William Peter Blatty's exorcism actually took place, the kids took one of the teachers onto the roof and threw him off, killing him. Maybe the revolution was beginning. I listened to WGMS, then called WQQW. They played a lot of Shostakovich and Prokofiev—Russian, Communist composers. The music was so angry that I believed the revolution was going to come. And it did."

Igor Stravinsky's *The Rite of Spring* had infamously sparked riots upon its initial performances with its brazen use of atonality. In stark contrast to his beloved children's work *Peter and the Wolf*, Sergei Prokofiev also composed war sonatas, venting his anger at the Soviet regime. Fahey, inspired by these composers and seeing a way to tell stories without the trappings of language, began to trace out his own musical aspirations. Through the power and violence of Russian music he discovered concepts of dissonance, atonality, and drastic rhythmic shifts. He dreamed of destroying the structures that tormented him, hearing this in the reverberations of his tiny radio speaker. Finally, the music spoke a truth he could relate to.

But anger wasn't his only excessive emotion. He would be prone to fits of great joy, energy, and enthusiasm, too. His passions for what excited him were as severe as his hatred for what bothered him. His musical focus shifted in 1954 at the age of fifteen, when his favorite station changed formats to country and western. He started to hear records like Jimmie Rodgers's "Blue Yodel No. 7," a fiddle and acoustic guitar number lamenting a girl who left the singer so lonesome that he didn't know what to do. Fahey's reaction was immediate. "It reached out and grabbed me and it has never let go of me," he remembered. "I went limp. I almost fell off the sofa. My mouth fell open. My eyes widened and expanded. I found myself hyperventilating. . . . I screamed for help but nobody was around and nobody came. Nothing has ever been the same since." Inspired and moved by those sounds coming through the radio, Fahey decided to pick up a seventeen-dollar Sears & Roebuck guitar. He earned the money by taking up a local paper route.

On summer nights he walked the streets of Takoma Park, exploring the boundaries of his neighborhood, which included a trash collection site near which several low-income families lived, less than a mile from his own house. One night he ran into an older black musician named Elmer Williams, who lived down on Prince George's Avenue. He was picking a guitar in a Blind Boy Fuller style. Soon Williams would teach Fahey how to play the twelve-bar blues in E. It was Fahey's first-ever encounter with a black musician. Every summer Friday night there would be giant outdoor crab boils in the mixed part of town. Fahey recalled going once and hearing Williams play for hours at these parties while neighbors and guests danced hypnotically in the street.

Like many lonely teenagers he found playing guitar an ideal activity, because it required no one else. He sat in his room with his instrument for hours on end. Feeding his newfound musical habit, he set out on a mission to find any information he could about music of all kinds, picking up musical techniques and ideas where he could. The first step was trying to track down a copy of the song he couldn't get out of his head, "Blue Yodel No. 7." Few people had any interest in or knowledge of this music, which barely existed in physical form. Asking around school, he heard about a young record collector named Dick Spottswood, a popular kid two years Fahey's senior who had friends in many different circles. Spottswood had a far different high school experience than Fahey. Indeed, not everyone who sought out such music was as tormented as he was. "When we were still in our teens the road ahead was filled with choices. We were lucky. We were kids getting good educations," Spottswood says. Fahey seemed troubled and disgruntled, while Spottswood was far more amiable and well adjusted.

"We had mutual friends who introduced us," recalls Spottswood. "He gave off very much a tall, tough-guy image. He dressed in T-shirts with the cigarettes rolled up in the sleeve and a toothpick in the mouth—that kind of thing. He had long black hair. He was very good-looking in a tough, blue-collar kind of way. At least that was the image he gave out. When I came to know him I could see behind the façade, but that's what he wanted to show to the world."

The two became friends, and together they would listen to bluegrass artists like Bill Monroe, while Fahey drank enough Coca-Cola to kill a normal man. Fahey would drive the pair to local thrift stores and soon beyond, up to Baltimore to hunt for records. Spottswood noticed that his new friend seemed to be suffering a great deal from his home life: "He was subject to such mood swings. He was depressed a good bit of the time, and at times when he was on the other side of the spectrum his enthusiasms threatened to carry him off," he says.

Although the suburbs were planned for families, kids had few desirable options for spending their free time. For a while Fahey hung out at the local pool hall with some greaser kids, but ultimately he knew he didn't fit in there. There was nothing there to stimulate his growing existential concerns. Through the Episcopal Youth Fellowship at Trinity Episcopal Church he found a refuge from the banality he saw around him, as well as a safe haven for intellectual and theological conversation. Away from the high school socialites, he put aside his tough-guy act and revealed a more pensive side. Attending an Episcopal church also doubled as rebellion against his Catholic father. There he met Anthony Lee, who played organ at services. Lee was a self-described awkward teenager and happily adopted the nickname Flea. "My first impression of John was simply that he was weird, which appealed to me because I was considered weird too," remembers Lee. At the time, Lee was a closeted homosexual and naturally a target in the repressive environs of 1950s suburbia. But Fahey, no stranger to ridicule from his strict father, did nothing to defend him. Lee recalls that "Fahey and I never hung out anywhere except at Trinity and at his home, primarily because he was ashamed to be seen in my company by his hard-rock friends, in whose presence, at Trinity Church, he mercilessly ridiculed me." Fahey, though deeply sensitive, had a sadistic side; he was able to target people's vulnerabilities, a trait gleaned from his father.

Fahey was attracted by Lee's musicianship, and their friendship grew over a shared absurd sense of humor and a mutual love of the wildly experimental music of composer Harry Partch. Lee's aunt had briefly dated Partch (although later he came out as gay) in the 1920s and he sent her a copy of his self-released album *Plectra and Percussion Dances* when she told him of her nephew's interest in modern music. Lee played it for Fahey and they both loved it. Partch was an artist who invented his own one-of-a-kind instruments to play avant-garde, microtonal works that followed few recognizable patterns. Once, as a prank, Fahey and Lee played a typically bizarre Partch record through the church PA system—much to the confusion of the attendees. On the organ, Lee would occasionally try to incorporate melodic phrases from gospel standards like "Uncloudy Day" in improvised sections of the hymns while Fahey would smirk from the pews.

By 1956, Fahey and Lee began attending St. Michael's Episcopal Church, which was just down the street from where Fahey now lived with his mother. Having been introduced by Spottswood, who also attended St. Michael's, Fahey found a group of suburban rebels, all of whom played music and talked about the malaise of being a teenager during the Eisenhower administration. There were even some girls. Among them was a young flute player named Nancy McLean. McLean was serious about her music studies, having taken private lessons from the first-chair flutist in the US Marine Corps band. A few years younger than the rest, McLean looked older than her age—an advantage at thirteen—and was drawn to what she saw as self-assured and interesting young people. She went to Northwestern High School in nearby Adelphi, the same school Fahey attended. "John portrayed himself as an outcast/outlaw/beatnik/pre-hippie," remembers McLean. "He was super cool in the way he walked, and rarely showed any true distress." However cool he presented himself, she saw that his erratic behavior at times could become provocative. She recalled Fahey would shout absurdities during inappropriate times at church such as "Being *is!*" and fall into fits of hysterical laughter. "One would have thought he was fox crazy with a few odd proclivities—nothing serious," she recalls. Spottswood saw similar traits in Fahey, and felt that his pranks and posturing were part of his appeal. "John managed to be charming by being anticharming," Spottswood says. "John was a contrarian; he always cared a lot but acted as if he didn't. He was never happier than when he was pulling your leg, although if you played a trick on him he could get extremely upset."

On Sundays the church would have potluck lunches, where young and old engaged in long discussions regarding religion. Fahey enjoyed being treated like an intellectual equal by adults. Spottswood had started his first year at the University of Maryland and was living in a spare room in St. Michael's pastor's house. During this time, Fahey and McLean started to develop what she described as a "chaste" romance. The two dated briefly and had no hard feelings when they stopped. In this sanctuary, Fahey had found a place for himself among his new friends.

Fahey continued his deep fascination with the guitar. He spent hours alone working on the fundamentals and trying to copy what he heard on records and the radio. His progress came slow and was the result of intense focus. Playing guitar became meditative therapy, an outlet for his anger and a way to channel his imagination. Music also became a way for him to connect with people. Fahey, with the occasional help of McLean, would make impromptu recordings while hanging out at St. Michael's. In this group structure, Fahey used the church resources at his disposal to make his earliest demos. These primitive recordings would serve as blueprints for future work. Bluegrass and classical were the main types of music he listened to, but what he imagined had little to do with any traditional genre. His friends were all interested in music to varying degrees, but Fahey was generating his own unique ideas by combining various musical influences.

Relating to the intellectual appeal of classical music, the sadness of country and western, and the spirituality of hymns, he became interested in the transformative powers of each. He saw music as a conduit for emotion. The process was less important than the results, especially since Fahey lacked the patience for learning how to read or write music, instead imitating techniques he heard on records. Merging genres with a bold ambitiousness, he would eventually call his style "American Primitive," in reference to his untrained methods. Rather than being restrained by formal song structure, he tried to keep the feel of more abstract classical structures, while using familiar fingerpicking patterns found in country and bluegrass. He took ideas from the music he heard as source material for collage. "I learned a few country-western songs," said Fahey. "I bought a chord book, and right away I started writing my own stuff, which, nobody else did that, I don't know why. I had a big background in listening to classical music and I started trying to compose, like I was playing the guitar but I heard an orchestra in my head. So I was really composing for full orchestra, and of course I didn't know enough chords or harmonies yet, but I came up with some interesting stuff."

Despite developing his own style, he struggled to articulate his ideas. "I don't mean to demean his talent, which was quite remarkable, but I think he must have worked harder, in private, on his picking and fingering and composing than he let on," recalls McLean. "He was inventive musically. But because he couldn't read music, I think he was prevented from making an even bigger mark. He needed Tony 'Flea' Lee to help him tune his guitars."

In 1956, having graduated high school, Fahey started working at Martin's Esso, an all-night gas station located on the central intersection of University Boulevard and New Hampshire Avenue on the border of Takoma Park and Langley Park. He would often play pranks on those he attended. Lee remembered, "He would give people directions, sending them in about a ten-mile-long circle which brought them right back to Martin's Esso, where they would look in confusion at Fahey, who would smile cheerfully and wave to them as they drove by." Eugene "Ed" (his first and last initials) Denson, a mutual Takoma Park friend of Spottswood, remembers him from this post as well. "He was young and thin, and fond of saying 'Happy motoring' to the customers—this was an advertising slogan of the time, and seemed to baffle the customers," he says. Fahey felt comfortable there, king of his micro-universe, messing with the squares for kicks.

His position seemed to suit him, and he often recalled it among his favorite memories. "Martin's was the only thing open all night in the county," said Fahey. "I always invited the cops to stay as long as they wanted. 'You want some free batteries for your flashlight? Take them.' I got to know all the cops and they let me speed. I never got caught. It was just, 'Hi, Fahey.' I became a very important person for the only time in my life. I still dream about it. I have very nice dreams of going back and working all night at this gas station. I liked the responsibility. In the three years I had that gig not one quart of oil was ever missed on the inventory. I watched. I'm real good at watching things. And that was the main part of the job during the week. There was not much work to do." He would never know hard labor, like that of the impoverished, but for the suburbs this was blue-collar work, and he enjoyed what it entailed: an earnestness. He would sit out at night and play guitar and watch the nothing go by, listening for the B&O engine whistling off in the distance. This simplicity suited him and allowed his mind to wander through the complexities of his mental orchestras. Most important, he was left alone.

SUNFLOWER RIVER BLUES

"Canvassing in and around Washington and Baltimore, as far north as Havre de Grace [Maryland] and even Philadelphia, I found hundreds of hillbilly and race records. . . . Stump Johnson on Paramount doing 'I'll Be Glad When You're Dead You Rascal You' and 'West End Blues' by Louis [Armstrong]. . . . On Richie Avenue East, I found a Kokomo Arnold record and the Carter Family doing 'When the Roses Bloom Again in Dixieland.' See what I mean? I could go on and on like this."

—John Fahey, interview, 1998

When Fahey began listening to records, he had no idea what a record collector was. Record collecting was a secret fascination, coded in mailing lists printed in the back of small jazz and record-collector magazines. The most rare and sought-after collectibles sold for hundreds of dollars.

Harry Smith was a pioneer of folk music collecting, an established avant-garde filmmaker, ethnomusicologist, and all-around rabid hoarder of obscure texts and arts. One of his main interests was 78 RPM records, and soon he accumulated them by the thousands: Cajun, blues, jazz, gospel, and more. In 1947 Smith approached

Folkways Records head Moe Asch with a pitch to sell his collection to the label. Asch instead commissioned a six-LP set of Smith's favorite recordings among his collection, entitled the *Anthology of American Folk Music*. Released in 1952, the set was a precedent-setting catalyst of the emerging interest in ethnomusicology and the roots of American music, introducing new listeners to iconic artists like the Carter Family, Uncle Dave Macon, Charley Patton, and dozens more. In the coming decade, Bob Dylan, Joan Baez, Johnny Cash, and many others found inspiration in the sounds introduced on the set. Smith and his *Anthology* showed that troves of cultural treasure were buried in America—in basements and attics, piled in boxes as trash.

Fahey initially rejected records by black musicians. After record hunting with Spottswood, he at first traded the blues records he found in exchange for country records. "Where I was brought up was very prejudiced towards Negroes," Fahey said. "I was taught to hate and fear them. I didn't like black music very much, I wouldn't even listen to it."

One day, while tallying their scores, Spottswood and Fahey played Blind Willie Johnson's "Praise God I'm Satisfied" to check the record's condition. It was 1957, and what Fahey heard changed him forever. He recalled, "I started to feel nauseated so I made him take it off, but it kept going through my head so I had to hear it again. When he played it the second time I started to cry, it was suddenly very beautiful. It was some kind of hysterical conversion experience where in fact I had liked that kind of music all the time, but didn't want to. So, I allowed myself to like it."

Spottswood's firsthand accounts mirror Fahey's own telling. "He went from disliking it quite a bit to adopting it totally in the span of a couple of hours. That's the surprising part to me, that that conversion was so much like Saul on the way to Damascus. It was as if lightning had struck. In the afternoon that predilection was not there, but in the evening it was the start of the rest of his life."

The song tells of a man thanking the Lord for saving him and clearing the clouds away, the joy of religious devotion echoing in Johnson's raspy voice. The music of bluesmen like Charley Patton and Blind Blake—other names he found in similar record scores—sent Fahey spiraling toward more collecting and research. Their guitar playing attracted him, Patton for his energetic and percussive playing and Blake for his sophisticated fingerpicking technique. What they had in common was syncopation.

Fahey related the anger he found in blues music to his own childhood angst. He heard the alienation of outsiders, voices that were ignored and absent from his own world. He felt removed and powerless in the suburbs and related his own complaints to the blues themes of loneliness and disappointment.

Fahey also found techniques he could use to further develop his guitar language. He taped his favorite records, keeping the recordings for reference and selling the physical records when he could fetch a nice price for them. Like many musicians, he began by studying his idols and playing along to their songs. Among his favorite artists was fingerpicking guitar player Sam McGee, a regular at the Grand Ole Opry known for his lightning-fast playing. Skip James was another player Fahey idolized, although very few James recordings were known at the time. Fahey found them to be among the most deeply affecting records of the blues canon.

The only way for Fahey to satisfy his emerging need for records was to go out and find them. Searching out old 78s in playable condition became a treasure hunt. There was no other way to hear the original country blues music. No radio stations played it, and record labels hadn't yet reissued blues music on the modern 33⅓ or 45 RPM formats.

Blues music was generally regarded as outdated, no longer of interest to current audiences. To people Fahey's age it was all but unknown. Blues fans had largely moved on to the electric R&B coming from Chicago from artists like Muddy Waters and the rest of the Chess Records roster. With bass, drums, and electric guitar added to the mix, the music took on a propulsive rhythm that set the tone for the coming rock 'n' roll onslaught. By contrast, country blues, with its scratchy acoustic guitars, already sounded antiquated by the mid-1950s. For a handful of young white teens in Maryland, however, it provided a glimpse into another reality, the dark gauze of pops and static only adding to the mystery. Living in suburban Maryland suddenly had a new advantage in its proximity to the South. The closer they could get to the source, the more likely there would be records to be found.

After exhausting their resources locally, Fahey and Spottswood began making long trips to the Deep South to find unheard gems, Fahey driving them in his '55 Chevy. Listening to Charley Patton records, they would hear lyrics with the names of towns such as Clarksdale, Mississippi, so they resolved to head to those places to hunt for 78s. Fahey, Spottswood, and occasionally others, including Lee, would often canvass poor black neighborhoods. Beyond looking in secondhand stores, the young white men would literally go door to door, looking for dusty old records whose owners no longer wanted them. These requests were such a breach of the racial divide at the time that the residents were wary of the visitors. But the potential danger in their pursuit did not deter Fahey and Spottswood. And they found often the locals were only too happy to sell their old junk. To these small-town folk, Fahey evidenced a looseness that most likely protected him, according to Lee.

"He would walk through the rural Southern black ghettos waving an old 78 and yelling, 'Got any old phonograph records? Buyin' up old records!'" Lee remembered. "Occasionally, whether out of discouragement or just ordinary insanity, he really would yell, 'Got any old arms or legs you'd like to sell? Buyin' up old arms and legs!' It's been suggested that one of the reasons he managed to survive unscathed from being a conspicuously white presence in the rural black South at a time when civil rights workers were being murdered by local police for such audacity, was simply that white racists, if they noticed him at all, probably dismissed him as too crazy to bother with."

About one house in ten would have some records, and most seemed willing to part with them. Generally they would pay around 25 cents a record. One of Fahey's most valued finds turned out to be the only known existing copy of Charley Patton's "Tom Rushen Blues" / "Pea Vine Blues" on Paramount. An old woman in Clarksdale, Mississippi, agreed to let him into her house and began to play a stack of records, talking about each one. When she reached a Charley Patton record, she began to tell a story about him, as Patton had lived in Clarksdale himself. Fahey cut her off, pretending to be disinterested. He didn't want her to know how much he coveted the record. He badgered her into a sale, wanting to abscond with his treasure before she could reconsider. Fahey, overwhelmed by his good fortune, gloated about his discovery. Unfortunately, whatever biographical or anecdotal story she might have imparted was now lost to the ages in his haste to secure the deal.

His sympathies and politics were naive, and they remained undeveloped despite his repeated trips to the South. All he saw was the music; the realities of poverty and institutionalized racism were far from his mind. Fixated on the musical expressions of the underclass, he expressed no regrets about their condition. His fantasy was of the Buddha-like bluesman who transcended the slums. Lee recalls Fahey's attitudes during an early canvassing trip: "Fahey's idea of how the South should be was so strongly stratified that whenever he saw a Negro family living in anything like human conditions he snorted in halfhearted resentment because he knew he wouldn't find any old records in such houses. 'Goddam white niggers!' he would say." Fahey acted as if he were myopically concerned with music, playing up his tough-guy image to his friends with provocative racist comments. But this front masked fear rather than hatred. The hardships of the impoverished and ignored, as represented through the records, spoke to him more than he was ready to admit.

After unearthing a few major discoveries, Fahey and his friends became sellers, buyers, and traders in an obscure world. There were only a handful of collectors in the DC metro area and they had come to know each other quite well. Spottswood was more interested in collecting than selling, amassing a gigantic catalog of prewar American music. "Today we have a pretty good idea of the breadth and scope of the commercial sound recordings of the 1920s, but in those days we were still discovering things," recalls Spottswood. "I would stockpile everything, but John would turn around and sell them if he needed money."

To cement his reputation and better capitalize on his finds, occasionally Fahey destroyed extremely rare records he found but which he already had, just to make his own copy more valuable. It was an act of selfishness he'd later regret. Fahey would often sell records to subsidize his canvassing trips. The records were auctioned by mail, after being strictly graded for condition, through private mailing lists. He had many buyers in New York City, at least three of whom formed a record label, the Origin Jazz Library, which started reissuing compilation albums of songs from old 78s in 1962. Notably, they introduced Skip James's "Devil Got My Woman" to a new audience on their *Really! The Country Blues 1927–1933* collection.

Spottswood's Zen calm was the inverse of Fahey's wild enthusiasm. "The records represented the art and that was the only way you could experience it," Spottswood says. "There weren't any people playing this music anymore. It was the only way to access the sound of a generation that had already passed. We white kids were experiencing them for the first time, because our parents had ignored that music totally." Spottswood later worked with the Library of Congress on the fifteen-LP series *Folk Music in America*, funded by a grant from the National Endowment for the Arts. Other scholars had previously examined the indigenous music of America, most notably Alan Lomax with his work through the Smithsonian recording folk and blues musicians. Though there had been research into the vast numbers of 78s pressed in earlier decades, many discoveries still remained to be made. The excitement of the unknown propelled Fahey and Spottswood forward.

Fahey heard in the blues a rage not expressed elsewhere, and stories fascinated with death, violence, and sex. "The reason I liked Charley Patton and those other Delta singers so much was because they were angry," Fahey remembered. "Their music is ominous. Patton had a rheumatic heart and he knew that he was going to die young, which he did. In Son House you hear a lot of fear. In Skip James you hear a lot of sorrow, but also a lot of anger. . . . I played some of the records to the doctor and he said, 'These guys are angry as hell.' "

Fahey started to incorporate blues techniques and melodic fragments into his own guitar work. With his heavy thumb he alternated the bass on the sixth and fourth or fifth and third strings of the guitar while his middle and ring fingers picked out a melody. He then would use bent notes and slides to mimic the vocal phrasings of the blues. This combination gave his playing a richly dynamic sound, with lead, rhythm, and melody all incorporated into a single instrumental performance. Though Blind Blake, Sam McGee, and Mississippi John Hurt all utilized similar techniques, Fahey fused them with his interest in dissonant modernism, taking his music somewhere else entirely.

Back at home, Fahey and Spottswood would make frequent trips to visit fellow country and blues collector Joe Bussard, another collector of the same age who lived in nearby Frederick. Gospel, blues, and hillbilly country records from the 1920s and '30s were his specialty. Along with various other collectors, they would hang out in Bussard's basement, listen to records, and trade their finds. Few young people had similar tastes, so Fahey, Bussard, and Spottswood enjoyed the chance to share with each other and talk shop.

By that time, home electronics had also emerged as a hobby, and many kids in the 1950s built their own transistor radios. Bussard made a lathe cutting machine at home and cut records one at a time from his basement. He'd even draw his own center labels by hand. Bussard greatly admired Fahey's guitar playing and asked to record him. He instructed Fahey to sing as rough as he could—so he would sound like a real bluesman. On these early home recordings, Fahey is heard singing far off key. As a singer, he seems hesitant and affected, as if trying to sound more withered and aged, or at other times simply laconic, covering songs by his newfound idol Charley Patton like "Some Summer Day."

Under the pseudonym Blind Thomas, Fahey cut six sides for Bussard's personal Fonotone label. For the most part, the recordings were just for fun. The actual market for such 78s was microscopic, as Bussard primarily did trades through the mail with other collectors and obsessive types. He also hosted a bluegrass radio show, on which he sold his Fonotone records for one dollar apiece on the air. Fahey, too, loved the idea of fooling some hopeless collector. That was the cover at least; but underneath the joke a more serious desire began brewing. Fahey always insisted that the recordings were inferior, never meant to be released, and never meant much to him. However, there are traces of what would become his seminal style, a heavy thumb keeping the rhythm and a richly melodic sense with minimal embellishments. It's hard to say if Fahey's voice was just genuinely poor or if he just never really tried, but Bussard's recordings were his first and last serious recorded attempts at singing.

The Fonotone recordings provide a template for the American Primitive style and are also an early example of a private press record label, a concept that came to greater fruition decades later. Knowing no one would be interested in their goings-on, the pressure was off Fahey and Bussard, and the records were made largely for their own enjoyment. But Fahey found a voice for himself through this process. What he liked so much about the original blues he couldn't find in the revivalists. Artists like Ramblin' Jack Elliott were releasing albums of finger-picked acoustic guitar and singing traditional folk songs such as "Salty Dog" or covering the Woody Guthrie catalog. "They're coming from people who lived the lives of folk people," Fahey said of the original songs from the *Anthology of American Folk Music*, "not from some suburbanite who's singing someone else's tradition. He can't figure out how to express himself on his own. It might be interesting if they expressed the anguish of the suburbs but they didn't. It would be authentic if that's what a suburbanite talked about and sang about. The pathos of the suburbs or whatever. But they didn't do that. Believe me, there's a lot of pathos there but instead they adopted other cultures' music which they didn't know anything about."

In 1960, Fahey entered his first year at the University of Maryland at College Park for a philosophy degree. He then quickly transferred to American University in Washington, DC, where he studied religion and philosophy, both natural fits for his aptitudes. "He had gotten his degree in philosophy at American University and he did some hard and honest work there," says Spottswood. "John was someone who had anti-intellectual tendencies but he was fairly intellectual." By then he had ditched his teen tough-guy act and started to ease up on his friends. "He had matured dramatically," recalls Lee. "He had stopped hanging around with a pack of half-witted, socially misfit punks, had been accepted as an intellectual equal by the adults at St. Michael's, and had begun to be recognized musically. So, having a more secure sense of himself, he began treating me more decently."

He also attended group therapy sessions with other parishioners, in which he presumably talked about his family issues. Fahey's connection to religion was based largely on this social acceptance and intellectual equality—on being treated like an adult. He took melodies from the hymnal and incorporated them into his playing. The priests who resided at St. Michael's had what was at the time a forward-thinking mentality toward young people, according to Lee: "John was influential in getting me my first church organist job at St. Michael's, roughly summer of 1960, when the rectorate was just changing from Don Shaw to Don [Donald Wylie] Seaton," Lee remembers. "Seaton would have left St. Michael's some time before 1966 and gone to Christ Church in Southeast DC, where I smoked dope in his rectory while we listened to *Sgt. Pepper's Lonely Hearts Club Band* [released June 1967]—a very hip priest, in other words."

Fahey continued collecting records, and socialized, drank, and played music with his friends. He and Spottswood at times played guitar and harmonica respectively at college parties in DC. Fahey often played with his back against the door so no one could leave the room while they were performing. This activity was at first purely recreational, but Fahey soon found something more to propel him.

THE LEGEND OF BLIND JOE DEATH

> "You're not meant to feel miserable in American society; you're supposed to keep the smile up. With *Blind Joe Death* I was secretly throwing hatred and death back in the faces of those people who told me I was bad and sinful because I had these feelings."
>
> —John Fahey, interview, 1998

John Fahey needed to properly document and share his music, and he had no intention of waiting for anyone else to do it for him. Inspired by Bussard, Partch, and others, he decided to create his own record label. Record plants often had special products divisions, which would do short runs of private (vanity) pressings in order to keep their machines calibrated in between larger runs of their own label's stock. Encouraged by this practice, Fahey self-released his first album, *Blind Joe Death*, in a pressing of 100 copies in 1959. He called his label Takoma Records in homage to his hometown. The record was packaged in a plain white sleeve with the words JOHN FAHEY printed on one side and BLIND JOE DEATH on the other.

The album borrowed liberally from his favored artists. Then, many blues and country songs were based on traditional arrangements, and the practice of adapting other artists' material was common in both genres. Fahey's album begins with "On Doing an Evil Deed," a piece Fahey claimed to have written about a girl whose heart he had broken. It contains elements of Robert Johnson's "Kind Hearted Woman Blues," and is played in standard tuning, in the key of A. It showcases Fahey's melodic fingerpicking runs and evolves over its five-minute duration, with Fahey bending notes on the refrain to add further dynamics. The album continues with a version of "St. Louis Blues." Originally composed by W. C. Handy, Fahey's adaptation channels a 1927 version recorded by the old-time duo Weaver and Beasley in its pacing.

Later, he picks up the tempo on his take of the classic folk song "John Henry," using a strange countermelody in the bridge to create some modern dissonance. He features some original compositions as well, including the melancholy "Sligo River Blues," an ode to the Sligo Creek of his Takoma Park childhood. Fahey wrote about the song in his liner notes, showcasing his emerging surreal literary voice: "An attempt to reconstruct an old song from three lines imperfectly remembered by an old peasant woman in the village of Balysodare, Sligo, who often sings them to herself. 'Every hand is lunatic that travels on the Moon.'"

A hint at Fahey's longer-form compositions is "The Transcendental Waterfall," another original song that takes a profound leap away from standard blues and country, using nonresolving chords in the manner of composers such as Bartok and Stravinsky. The piece has an abstract form, not locked into the standard rhythm of the other album tracks. On his traditional blues, Fahey keeps a heavy lock on the structure, but on this track Fahey explores texture and improvisation, placing fragments of riffs together in an unorthodox manner, using strange bends to twist notes into unusual territory. With a few harmonic taps the piece departs even further from the blues standards and succeeds, creating an altogether new sound for acoustic guitar.

Although the playing remains hesitant at times, like on his Fonotone records, *Blind Joe Death* demonstrates the emergence of a unique voice. While other guitarists such as Dave Van Ronk were picking blues and country, no one else explored such a mixture of modern elements. For an album with no vocals, *Blind Joe Death* speaks a different language.

Having studied the details of the blues, Fahey now had the template to create his own persona. While Blind Thomas had been a start, the full realization of Fahey's alter ego emerged in his new, bolder character, Blind Joe Death. He reflected on the name with alternating accounts. Depending on when and by whom he was asked, his answers varied wildly. If feeling shy, he distanced himself from any serious intent: "When I made my first record I thought it would be a good joke to have me on one side, have the label say 'John Fahey' on one side, and this guy 'Blind Joe Death' on the other side . . . Also I was thinking, whenever you print the word 'Death' people look at it, and I was thinking of record sales already even though I was only going to have a hundred copies pressed."

Among his friends, reactions to his alter ego were mixed. Some recognized Fahey's conflicted feelings regarding his own credibility. Part of the appeal of an alias was being able to hide behind the signifiers of blues culture. With this cloak, he could obscure the fact that the music was made by a white suburbanite. Spottswood agrees the duality existed from the beginning: "I think he was trying to have it both ways. Having adopted that music and attempted to play it, I think he also wanted a badge of authenticity, which of course he wasn't ever going to have, because he was learning that music secondhand from records. In order to create some authenticity attached to him, he created a mythical person."

Fahey wasn't playing the blues, but rather a deviated form based on blues structures. He wasn't trying to tell anyone else's story; he had his own experiences to express. And he followed his passions with a fierce intensity. The darker side of Blind Joe Death, according to Fahey, is the embodiment of all the hate and negativity rippling under the surface of the faux suburban dream. While Fahey, as a child, was powerless, Blind Joe Death projects from a position of power, lashing out against those who repressed and abused him. From behind this veil, Fahey expresses his contempt for society. As an artist whose repertoire is instrumental, Fahey has a wealth of things he expresses with his imagery. "The whole point was to use the word 'death,'" said Fahey. "I was fascinated by death and I wanted to die. I probably could have told you that at the time, but I wasn't being that honest. Blind Joe Death was my death instinct. He was also all the Negroes in the slums who were suffering. He was the incarnation, not only of my death wish, but also of all the aggressive instincts in me." Through Blind Joe Death, Fahey created a minstrelized persona. These revelations came later, however; at the time the symbolism was seen as largely tongue in cheek.

Stylistically, there was no distinction between the music on each side of *Blind Joe Death*; it all sounded of a piece. The recordings have a homemade feel, enhancing the intimacy of the performances with its pops and imperfections. The bare aesthetic of the packaging matched the music. He sold the record mostly at his all-night gas station post. Occasionally he would drop copies in local thrift stores. It took three years for him to get rid of them all. Few imagined that it would have such far-reaching and long-lasting effects.

One of the few copies that Fahey sent out was to folk/blues scholar and producer Sam Charters. Known for his production work, Charters made his name recording ethnomusicology records for the Folkways label in the 1950s. Charters, also a scholar, had written one of the earliest books on the blues, the seminal *The Country Blues*, published in 1959. Fahey respected Charters's work and hoped to find a sympathetic ear. But upon initial listen, Charters recalled being less than impressed. Guitarists like Dave Van Ronk were acclaimed for their startling prowess, however these players usually sang as well. Charters had worked with accomplished guitar players such as Bahaman Joseph Spence, whose fierce yelp and hard attack sounded unlike any other, as well as electric blues icon Muddy Waters. To Charters, Fahey's record sounded generic. "When John sent me the record, it sounded like a lot of stuff I'd already heard and played. I didn't think it was that special and I sent him a letter saying so," says Charters. The letter upset Fahey greatly and their relationship began on a sour note.

Spottswood was equally unimpressed: "I didn't think his technique was very sophisticated. He basically played in a variety of open tunings and that was part of his appeal, that you could pick up the guitar and play like him if you wanted to as it wasn't that difficult." While these criticisms were valid, they did nothing to deter Fahey, and his playing continued to develop privately.

Ed Denson felt differently. Another participant in the burgeoning Maryland blues-collector circles, he picked up on Fahey's talents early on. He wasn't a musician, but he championed the talents he found around him. He was among the first to foresee the massive appeal of Fahey's music. Denson had explored psychedelic drugs and was starting to become interested in left-wing politics. A sharp, laconic guy with a penchant for writing like Samuel Beckett in his creative writing classes, Denson was a regular around the folk hangouts. "Fahey could play virtually any piece on a 78, in the style of any of the older artists," says Denson. "His guitar playing, especially on record, took the music and moved it into another realm, so he too was not 'authentic,' but I don't think that disturbed him. John never expressed any sense of his own feelings about his own music to me that I recall. He did what he did, and from the first time I met him, he was good enough at it to perform to audiences and issue records."

By 1960, Fahey was playing at informal events at the Unicorn on 17th and S Streets down in Washington, DC. The club hosted a hootenanny every Friday, which would attract all the local kids just getting into the folk scene. Fahey's music, containing elements of blues and country, sounded familiar to them, but its instrumental focus was unlike the rambling stories of the common folk guitarist. Even from his first performances, the music resonated with audiences.

Max Ochs, a classmate of Denson's, first encountered Fahey at the Unicorn. A fellow guitar player, Ochs also performed at the hangouts. He recalled Fahey's commanding presence having an immediate impact on those around him. "He was not chatty," remembers Ochs. "He had a larger-than-life demeanor that inspired a kind of hero worship in me. I was a devotee, sitting on the floor as one of a circle of devotees around a blues bodhisattva. He sat in the chair in the center of the room and he played his latest compositions, sometimes sounding as if they were being created as he played, all with an expressionless mask, a deep looking inward." Fahey connected the blues to his darker thoughts, and this resonated with his audience. "My impression was that there was an old, old sorrow in John Fahey that a quart of whiskey might assuage but never alleviate," adds Ochs, "an affect that we were decades too early to think might indicate the presence of some pathology, like autism. We were more disposed to

ON THE SUNNY SIDE OF THE OCEAN

"I remember when you'd go into a folk store, there'd always be a big sign up, 'Should Pete Seeger Go To Jail?' I'd always say, 'Absolutely. Because he sings such lousy music.'"

—John Fahey, interview, 1994

Propelled by desire, Fahey headed west, with unrequited love as his blinders. Ed Denson and Pat Sullivan had moved to California to pursue their graduate degrees. Fahey followed suit and in the fall of 1963 enrolled in the master's program in philosophy at the University of California, Berkeley, where Pat was also studying. Her marriage to Denson would be short-lived. She would leave a trail of broken hearts all through the Berkeley music scene.

In Berkeley, as Denson recalls, "John and I lived in one large, somewhat ramshackle residence out in the sticks beyond Clayton. I don't know if Pat was there or not. My only really clear memories of that period are of the Clayton Peacock"—a bird that frequently appeared on the property.

Fahey continued his pursuits as both a student and musician, with aspirations to write a scholarly thesis on the blues. His expertise in the once extremely marginal field was in vogue now that interest in it had started to go mainstream. The folkies were especially interested in the blues' cultural relevancy in the era of civil rights. Fahey was already far ahead of those who were just beginning to listen, and his considerable knowledge become another source of his charisma. "Among these people, John was a person who had done the things they were trying to do. He was an excellent guitarist, and his persona suggested that he knew something they did not—which was, in a way, true," Denson says. Unlike many others, Fahey was often vocal with his criticisms. And however much he abused them, he still found followers drawn to his strange personality. "I would not say there was anything endearing about John, even in his vulnerabilities, but for people of a certain personality type, there was something attractive. . . . 'I'm always surrounded by midgets,' he said one day. He was tall, but the reference was to accomplishments, not height," recalls Denson.

Despite the tension regarding Pat, Denson and Fahey remained amicable and were able to seemingly ignore the situation. The two decided to relaunch Takoma Records as a full-time independent record label dedicated to the guitar, with Fahey as its cornerstone artist. Fahey was fortunate to have found a partner who possessed all the networking, organizational, and social skills that he lacked. Through Denson, Fahey was able to market his music to the new folk audience. They never much discussed Pat, or even Fahey's music, and the partnership, for the time being, worked out. "My relationship with John was not unpleasant, nor stormy," remembers Denson. "Generally speaking he was happy to record music, and I was happy to get it on the market and hope to sell it."

Independent, artist-owned labels were uncommon at the time. An important distinction between Fahey and other contemporary instrumentalists was his realism. He knew no label would be interested in putting out instrumental guitar music; so he simply took matters into his own hands and pressed records, in limited quantity, himself. This self-reliance cemented his commitment, while others simply waited to be discovered. With Denson's help, Takoma Records would blossom into a sizeable and venerable record label. They soon began plotting other artists to recruit.

The most coveted country blues recordings had been made in the late 1920s and early 1930s, and it was perfectly reasonable to assume that many of these performers were still alive, some perhaps even still playing. In March 1963, Tom Hoskins's discovery of Mississippi John Hurt got the ball rolling. There was no telling who else might still be out there. The logical next step for an academic and collector like Fahey was to look for the artists themselves while on collecting trips. Many of them were still hanging around the same haunts they referenced on their records thirty years earlier, completely unaware of any interest in their work. A shot-in-the-dark postcard to a small town in Mississippi started the process.

Bukka White originally recorded for the Victor label in the early 1930s. He was later convicted of murder and sent to prison. Famed folklore documentarian Alan Lomax made several recordings of White while in prison, and White received recognition during the early 1960s folk movement when Bob Dylan covered his song "Fixin' to Die Blues" on his first album. In the process, White became introduced to the folk music community as a pioneer. To these middle-class, white teenagers who made up the folkie crowd, White represented authenticity.

After hearing White sing about Aberdeen, Mississippi, on his records, Fahey sent a postcard to Bukka's attention care of general delivery to the Aberdeen Post Office, offering him $100 to record for Takoma. White lived in Tennessee, where he was employed at a tank factory. By sheer chance, his cousin worked at a Mississippi post office and forwarded the letter to him, and White responded to the upstart label.

White was a fast-talking, good-natured character. After visiting him at his home in rural Tennessee, Fahey formed a deep bond with him, not only through music but also through their mutual fascination with trains. White told stories of riding the rails, a prospect that had thrilled Fahey dating back to his Maryland days, the sounds of the B&O still resounding in his memories. White indulged in tales of the old times and would take Fahey fishing when Fahey would come to visit him. All the while the two would drink whiskey like water. White also indulged Fahey in fictional tales of Charley Patton. When White ultimately agreed to record for Takoma, Denson and Fahey had their dreams, to a large extent, realized.

However, even with the common bonds of music, cultural differences soon became pronounced. Many old bluesmen and their young white sponsors had difficulty trusting each other in regard to money. Often the attention generated from the press did little to sell LPs in mass quantities and the financial rewards were slow in coming. In a letter Fahey sent to Sam Charters dated November 27, 1963, he writes, "There is a slight chance Bukka will break my contract and go away and at this point he's been so much trouble that I don't think I'd mind too much if this occurred." According to Charters, Fahey had to hide in doorways in Memphis from an angry White, who thought Fahey owed him money. White only recorded one album for Takoma, yet he and Fahey remained friends for years afterward—once the unpleasantness of their business had been settled.

Takoma Records was launched in earnest with the release of Bukka White's *Mississippi Blues* and John Fahey's second album *Death Chants, Breakdowns and Military Waltzes*. Much to everyone's surprise, Fahey's record sold more quickly, with the help of new distributor Norman Pierce, who sold Takoma albums direct to stores. *Death Chants* was sold out in just a matter of weeks.

Four years had passed since he released *Blind Joe Death*. A tongue-in-cheek press release from Takoma read as follows:

> John recorded his second LP, saddened that Death was not there to share in a triumph that was as much his as anyone's. The extent of that triumph may be seen in the fact that our Directors, without hesitation, issued (in part) the following statement in a June press conference: It is a measure not only of the tremendous gain in maturity, stature, and international reputation of Mr. Fahey, but of the vital and expanding folk market in this nation and across the seas, that we have, without president [*sic*], decided to issue an initial pressing of 300 copies of *Death Chants, Breakdowns and Military Waltzes*.

The album retained the same homemade look and feel as its predecessor: a white silk-screened sleeve with the words JOHN FAHEY in black and the album title below.

The music, however, featured far more confident performances and compositions. The opening strain of "Sunflower River Blues" is a mid-tempo fingerpicked anthem with a melancholy that echoes throughout the piece. The song is an ode to Charley Patton, written the year prior in Yazoo City, Mississippi. A unique element in the track is the use of an open-C tuning. Fahey's bottleneck skills inform the stirring "On the Beach of Waikiki," a song written in 1915, which is as hopeful and lively as anything Fahey ever performed. There are odes to his classical influences as well: in the opening measures of

"Stomping Tonight on the Pennsylvania/Alabama Border," he bor-
rows a riff, which alternates between a second-inversion C-major
chord and a second-inversion C-sharp minor chord, from the end of
Ralph Vaughan Williams's "Symphony No. 6." The same track quotes
both Skip James and the plainsong hymn "Dies Irae"—a pastiche of
influences and styles that brought out his obsession with death. The
brief, self-composed track "America" features a rare instance of Fahey
playing twelve-string guitar. The song uses harmonics and muted
strings to tap out its initial strains and then blooms into a lush refrain.
The album closes with a rendition of an Episcopal hymn.

With the musical developments of his second album, Fahey
started to enter the world of professional musicians. At the same time,
with the inclusion of his surreal and bizarre liner notes, he continued
to build on the farce he began with Blind Joe Death. He wrote about
himself, replete with made-up words and fictional places in a jumbled
yet fascinating narrative.

> John Fahey had made his first guitar from a baby's coffin, and led
> the old blind Negro [Blind Joe Death] through the back alleys and
> whore-houses of Takoma Park in return for lessons. When the Sec-
> ond World War broke out, John was already a musician in his own
> right. His career as a volk entertainer was briefly interrupted when
> he was drafted and sent to New Zealand to fight with the allies
> against the Finno-Armenian invasion. After the war was over, John,
> a decorated war hero, returned to his home and re-established rela-
> tions with Blind Joe. In 1952, only a few years before Blind Joe's
> bodily ascension, Patricia Sullivan working in co-ordination with
> the Library of Congress (of Bessarabia), recorded the two of them
> and issued them on the now rare Takoma label. . . . John Fahey
> went insane in 1964 and died shortly there after. He spoke to me
> in his last minutes on his dying bed and said: "Take down my old
> guitar and smash it against the wall so I can die easy." I did so and
> he passed away with a chthonic smile on his face.

His friends Lee, Spottswood, and McLean enjoyed these notes, as he often included allusions to each of them within the texts. It's never made clear who is speaking, the assumption being a noted scholar or critic, although the writing is credited to Chester Petranick, a former music teacher at Takoma Park schools.

In the time since his debut album, the market for his music, still seen under the banner of folk music, had expanded. The most famous outlet for the emerging cultural celebration of folk and blues was the Newport Folk Festival, which began in 1959 as an extension of the already successful Newport Jazz Festival. Promoter George Wein teamed with Folklore Productions' Manny Greenhill to organize a series of concerts catering to the rising popularity of the blues, country, bluegrass, and folk. By 1963, with attendance blossoming to 45,000, Newport was a celebration of the music and culture, providing workshops, panels, and over 100 performances over the weekend of July 26–28 of that year. Bob Dylan, Johnny Cash, and Joan Baez all performed at the fest alongside blues legends such as Mississippi John Hurt, who performed for their new public for the first time. As an expert historian and guitarist, Fahey attended the festival, participating in one of the smaller workshops. While the music, at times, engaged him, the politics left him absolutely cold, and he questioned the motivations of those involved.

Fahey famously criticized Pete Seeger during the festival's Topical Song Discussion workshop—an act of near sacrilege since Seeger was a sacred cow to the young activists. Having been jailed for his protest songs, Seeger seemed the living embodiment of a modern folk hero, an actual martyr. Fahey wasn't buying it. He voiced his opinion that the songs sung by Seeger did not represent the contemporary voice of the actual people. The actual folk were listening to R&B, and while they supported the civil rights cause, black audiences certainly weren't listening to the music of their past as reinterpreted by white intellectuals. In Fahey's eyes, white performers like Seeger didn't understand the blues, missing its emotional rawness. Never shy to express himself, he stood up against the zeitgeist, to mostly deaf ears. "I was trying to convince the audience, who was mostly Negros, that these jerks like Phil Ochs and Seeger were writing music about Negros to make money and not to help Negros," said Fahey. "That they were actually exploiters. And I got booed by the Negros. I kept saying, 'I think that Negros have enough intelligence to write their own songs. I'm really convinced of it.' BOO! I was set up, I just didn't know it." Fahey didn't consider himself or any other middle-class, educated white people as "folk." They were not the common people, and their enthusiasm to him seemed insincere.

The mystery of the blues continued to captivate Fahey as widespread interest in the subject grew. Out of all the lost bluesmen, Fahey searched for Skip James with the most interest. James remained perhaps the most elusive, his recordings among the most rare, and his material the most deeply sinister. His songs of murder, misogyny, and coldness were unsurpassed in their severity. His song "22-20 Blues," an ode to his pistol of choice, features the lyrics "Sometimes she gets unruly / An she act like she just don't wanna do / But I get my 22-20 / Cut that woman in two." Even for the blues, James's music contained a sadistic streak. James channels sorrow and anger, the feeling enhanced by his then-unknown open D-minor guitar tuning, which gives a more sullen tone than standard tuning, a haunting match for James's weary falsetto. His mystique among collectors grew as more of his records were uncovered and became coveted on the underground market.

A black cloud hangs over James's 1931 recordings, which bear intense themes of mortality and betrayal. But underneath the violence lies a deep remorse, with no less than the punishment of God to contend with. James, torn between the secular and the religious worlds, spent time as both a bootlegger and an assistant to his father, a Texas preacher. His father hated his music and forbade him to perform the blues while working at the church. James vacillated between these worlds, his own music and decadent lifestyle clashing with his religious upbringing. He played songs in praise of the Lord, such as "Jesus Is a Mighty Good Leader." This kind of duality—the struggle between sin and salvation—fascinated Fahey.

At first, Fahey romanticized the people behind those lost blues records as entities of magical proportions. Surely, if there were wisdom or answers, Skip James possessed them. Fahey imagined that finding James would be like finding a great spirit. In reality, few answers would be found. But Fahey was oblivious to all else in his path. He tackled his obsessions with great expectations. "I was seeking out mean, sadistic, aggressive, hateful, and maybe even dangerous expressions and expressers of music most cruel," said Fahey. "Because the search was urgent and of utmost importance. Because I had to find them, locate them, understand them (maybe not master them), but at least have some knowledge of their origins."

When another lost bluesman, Ishman Bracey, was found in Jackson, Mississippi, the discovery set off a flare for Fahey. Bracey and James had recorded for the same label at around the same time. Perhaps Bracey would have some knowledge as to the whereabouts of James. Fahey planned a trip to the Deep South to find out. He took friend and guitarist Bill Barth, as well as Frank Zappa guitarist and fellow Takoma Park native Henry Vestine—both blues scholars in their own right. After a long drive through the swamps of Mississippi, they spoke to Bracey, who gave them a hint: James lived somewhere near the town of nearby Bentonia. At the local gas station they found someone who knew James's wife. They discovered that James was in the hospital. It had been more than thirty years since James recorded music when Fahey, Barth, and Vestine found him in 1964 in a hospital in Tunica, Mississippi, suffering from testicular cancer. The three paid his medical bills so that he could be released.

Back at his home a few days later, James didn't offer so much as a thank-you. Barth had brought a guitar, and the sixty-two-year-old James, tuning it to open D minor, began shakily playing his classic songs. The odd chord structures and tuning were a revelation, as they had been trying to figure out the secret to his sound for years. Fahey hoped to record James for Takoma as well. He expected surprise and perhaps a bit of excitement from James, considering the lengths to which they had gone to find him. Indeed, Fahey's sense of connection to the music was so strong he considered James a mystical figure. But while James may have possessed a true understanding of misanthropy and darkness, he had no intention of helping Fahey unravel his problems. In Fahey's estimation, James remained an angry man. He bragged about his nefarious past and dismissed and insulted many of those whom he came across. Fahey would later proclaim in a somewhat bitter tone that he had "bought" James, surely aware of the racial implications of the statement. In Fahey's mind, James would have rotted to death in that hospital if not for his heroic and altruistic efforts.

James would never record for Takoma. "James became a frightful figure who inspired fear and loathing everywhere he went," recalled Fahey. "It was his attitude toward his music. Toward his audience. Toward himself. Toward everything. He made no attempt to disguise his disgust and disdain for people he met, the music that they played and liked and for his gigs. Everybody noticed it. James' connection to the unconscious was broken. He had nothing to teach anybody anymore."

Others sought to capitalize on and exploit the newly rediscovered bluesman, and some therefore doubted Fahey's motivations. Skip James biographer Stephen Calt details his take on Fahey's intentions: "Although the blues field in 1964 tended to attract people who could charitably be described as connivers, the petty nature of the burgeoning blues business obscured the fact that the real purpose of James' discoverers and sponsors was to make money off him."

The blues revival had an immediate impact on the contemporary music scene. James and legendary bluesman Son House both performed and were reintroduced to audiences at the 1964 Newport Folk Festival. (No one is sure if Fahey attended.) Skip James's comeback album *Today* ended up coming out on Vanguard Records, a label that had far more resources than Takoma. The British psychedelic rock band Cream covered his song "I'm So Glad," to great success. Photos of James and House were featured in *Newsweek* alongside an article on the blues revival. Little of this translated into direct record sales, but rock musicians had a new template.

"Those rediscoveries were earth-shaking to those of us who cared about them," says Denson. "If John had been offered the Nobel Prize for Bukka's discovery, I don't think we would have been surprised, so great was our sense of the importance of it. Perhaps it is better expressed as finding a new pyramid in Egypt, or a lost city in the Amazon. We were fully engaged in the projects, and believed that universal recognition for the artists was bound to come. In a way we were right: Robert Johnson got a stamp issued with him on it." Fahey was not possessive. Once James and White had embarked upon their revival careers, Fahey let them go their way and returned his focus to his own music.

Death Chants, Breakdowns and Military Waltzes helped propel Fahey further into the role of burgeoning guitar icon. Others outside his circle began to take notice. Peter Stampfel of the Holy Modal Rounders, an emerging group of experimental folk musicians, wrote favorably about the album in his column in *Boston Broadside* magazine. Given this new regional interest, Fahey was asked to play a weeklong residence at the Odyssey Coffee House in Boston for the sum of $200.

Other players were now beginning to add to the conversation of instrumental guitar. Another key figure in the early Takoma Records catalog was Robbie Bǎsho. Bǎsho grew up as Daniel R. Robinson Jr. in Baltimore, the adopted son of a middle-class family. He attended Catholic school, then military school, until he entered college in 1959 at the University of Maryland as a premed student. Far from a bookworm, Robinson defied the stereotype and spent some time working as a bouncer in a club. Known as an athletic, weightlifting jock, he transformed himself into a beatnik poet when he discovered the twelve-string guitar in his junior year. Robinson played the standard folk guitar repertoire of the time, which included the likes of the Kingston Trio, along with more pop-oriented material.

An encounter with the music of Ravi Shankar in 1962 set Robinson on an obsessive path toward Eastern music—Indian raga, specifically. To solidify this transformation he renamed himself Robbie Bǎsho, after the Japanese poet Matsuo Bashō. Bǎsho aimed to play solo steel-string guitar as elevated compositional music—not for pop songs—and began writing extended ragas for the instrument. Despite his prodigious skills on the guitar, his lack of social graces left him with few friends or supporters. He had no sense of humor about his work. Described as unapproachable and insufferable, no one seemed to like him.

"Fahey was obnoxious, but Bǎsho was just a nebbish—the personality of a frog," recalls Tom Weller, a regular on the Berkeley folk scene. "He often complained that he couldn't get laid." The folk movement championed a relation to the common man, but Băsho presented himself as a mystic and dressed in robes and capes. Convinced of his own importance, he viewed his music as having spiritual and magical properties. Băsho tried to channel divinity and Eastern thought through long-form fingerpicking that was stunning in its complex virtuosity. Leaving the blues behind, he followed his new path with religious dedication. "Băsho was a religious mystic who used his guitar for chanting and expression of his religious views," recalls Charters. "He didn't interact in our world at all except to ask for a great deal of praise. I didn't like him personally or musically, but Ed [Denson] liked the music a lot."

Another important distinction between Băsho and his peers was his over-the-top, operatic singing style. His overwhelming bravado turned off many—although some were blown away by his emotional conviction. Băsho seemed removed from Americana in all but instrumentation. Few were ready for his mix of instrumental, raga-influenced guitar, or his pretensions.

Naturally, a tension between Fahey and Băsho grew, as they shared the same management, label, and scene. An intense gunslinger competition developed between the two. Fahey naturally believed himself superior as a musician, because of his compositional abilities. Fahey thought so little of Băsho that he would sell Băsho's LPs at a deep discount at his shows. Later, Fahey would admit that Băsho had interesting moments, but for the most part he had nothing to do with him. "He was crazy," said Fahey. "I never hung out with Robbie personally much. Nobody did. You couldn't." Even so, the two guitarists would be the mainstays of the Takoma label, both releasing solo guitar LPs at regular intervals.

Băsho's 1965 Takoma Records debut LP, *The Seal of the Blue Lotus*, although largely ignored, became a cult classic to guitar players of a more experimental nature. Băsho played with a gorgeous, dexterous style, rife with dramatic flair and flourishes. By incorporating more Eastern influences the music came across as forward thinking, stylistically fitting the emerging Takoma style of innovative contemporary players. In early 1966, Băsho moved out to Berkeley, having been picked up by Denson and various members of Country Joe & the Fish, whom Denson was also managing, on their return from a cross-country journey. Not surprisingly, Băsho did not bond with his new West Coast contemporaries on the trip. The group stopped in the Sierra Nevada Mountains, excited about going out in the woods and enjoying the trees and nature while taking psychedelics. Băsho sat in the car and kept honking the horn, complaining that he needed to get back to Berkeley to see a doctor. A notoriously vocal hypochondriac, he complained constantly about back problems. In fact, Băsho would demand they stop at hospitals the whole trip. Not once could a doctor find anything wrong with the twentysomething Băsho.

Meanwhile, Fahey was busy establishing himself as a powerful figure in the music scene. With his encyclopedic knowledge of prewar American music and his biting wit he became a difficult man to win over when fans started to seek his approval. Still, despite his attitudes, he found devotees and fans who became so enthralled by his music that they forgave his often brash behavior. Fahey's approval became coveted among a certain group. "Once the records began selling even modestly he was, in our small circle, a star," recalls Denson about Fahey's charmless charisma. "He had achievements, and in his special area he was really one of the leading figures. Everyone around him was young—yet to achieve anything—and especially at that time of life, someone who is mysterious, accomplished, and who disdains people or work that you think is good, is impressive."

Back at home in the summer, Denson produced sessions for what would be Fahey's third album, *Dance of Death & Other Plantation Favorites*. Retaining the feel of its predecessors, the album continued to showcase Fahey's artistic and commercial growth. Still, Fahey remained a cult figure.

POOR BOY LONG WAY FROM HOME

"He said he was confused, because, he said, he couldn't get along with the women he liked. He was going to go up to see some psychoanalyst or something in Miricle Valley Arizojahi. I guess he did. I haven't seen him in months."

—John Fahey, in his liner notes to *Days Have Gone By*, 1967

The left-wing politics of the student movement was bringing attention to blues and folk as the soundtrack to the civil rights movement. Some of those who started coming to Fahey's shows were more interested in politics or drugs than music or records. Fahey hated them. To him, the student idealists had naive worldviews and dreamed of unrealistic political utopias. A bunch of college students sitting in parks singing "This Land Is Your Land" was enough to make him downright irate. "I hate mellow," he stated emphatically. "There are lots of other things, people, places and times and what-have-you that I hate, but nothing I hate so much as Berkeley in the 1960s."

When folk music became popular, Fahey was disappointed. He found the style, as popularized by groups like the Weavers, insufferable. Unsurprisingly, he considered those who played such music to be largely unsuitable as allies or friends. Others soon took note of his negative attitudes. Many had ventured west to find a more freewheeling, exotic lifestyle; they were ready to experiment and cast off the shackles of 1950s repression in the coming age of sexual revolution. But in Fahey's estimation, many of the musicians and fans lacked the ability to think critically and blindly followed popular trends. Always an iconoclast, Fahey found himself starkly at odds with the Berkeley scene.

So, in the fall of 1964, Fahey moved to Venice, California. Earlier that year, at the UCLA Folk Festival, he had met a like-minded scholar who believed in both the purity of bluegrass and the insincerity of the current folk scene. D. K. Wilgus had just been hired to start a new graduate program in folk studies at UCLA. Fahey was an ideal candidate, and Wilgus encouraged him to switch schools. Folk studies would offer him more than any of his previous academic experiences, and directly intersect with his music. The change would also provide an ideal opportunity to make the transition away from the town he despised so much.

Berkeley had offered him little in terms of intellectual stimulation, but there were personal reasons as well. After years of pursuit and hurt feelings, his on-and-off romance with Pat Sullivan finally came to a concrete conclusion. After her marriage with Denson had ended, she began dating Fahey. And for a short time, they lived together and he was joyously happy. She left him in a matter of months. Fahey was furious. During an angry conversation he threatened her, telling her that he was going to wait a year or two—until she least expected it—and then kill her. Frightened, she told university officials that he was stalking her. He tried to focus his energy on new hobbies such as karate. The school psychiatrist, after a few sessions, determined there was nothing medically wrong with him and suggested he reconnect with the church; he should become more proactive so that he could meet a nice girl whom he could marry and who would take care of him. This would be the end of Pat Sullivan in his life—although she would later be immortalized in his liner notes as "Evil Devil Woman."

Pat was a teenage fantasy, and Fahey had grown into a man. Once he became well known for his music, it was a boon to his personal life. He immediately attained a notable presence on the UCLA campus because of his emerging status as performer and recording artist. In addition, he finally had a place where he could seriously dive into his specific subject of expertise. He chose Charley Patton as the sole focus of his thesis. He would dissect Patton lyrically and musically, breaking down every verse, measuring and charting their structures.

One of Fahey's neighbors was Barry Hansen, a fellow classmate in the folklore program. Hansen had a vast record collection and later went on to a career as famed radio personality Dr. Demento. At UCLA, he became one of Fahey's closest supporters. Both were dedicated to their pursuit of rare music, so they naturally had a lot in common. Hansen's easy temperament and wacky sense of humor appealed directly to Fahey's sensibilities.

Hansen lived at 525 Grand Boulevard. The next lot south had three small houses, back to back. Fahey occupied the one in the middle: one room with a tiny kitchen and bathroom. The floor was usually littered with dozens of empty Coca-Colas. Fahey still drank it constantly, usually three quarts a day. At that time Venice was still considered a rough part of town, riddled with crime. The sounds of police sirens and bar fights often echoed through the streets. Fahey seemed oblivious to the chaos. "One time in Venice we were hanging out all night, drinking a lot. I like whiskey too," recalls Sam Charters. "I remember it was very dangerous where he lived. There was a whole line of police right on John's corner, hiding. There was a coffee shop there, and there were two bikers sitting in there talking about Sartre's existential theory. And that's what the cops were waiting for, these two bikers to come out. And there was John, living in the middle of all of this, people getting shot. In a way, he self-created a hell that he lived in."

Another member of their record-obsessed entourage was Alan Wilson. Wilson was a collector and guitarist Fahey met in Boston in the summer of 1965 while in town playing shows and recording songs for his album *The Transfiguration of Blind Joe Death*. Aside from music, they had a great deal in common. According to Rebecca Davis Winters's biography of Wilson, he was similarly troubled. Described as painfully shy, with a demanding father, Wilson had trouble socially. This was due in large part to his notorious lack of personal hygiene. He often had to be told by friends to change clothes or bathe, as he would never think to do so on his own. As such, he possessed a pungent body odor—even among the liberal, freewheeling set. Wilson existed mostly as a catatonic who lived on barely anything but focused so intently on the country blues and guitar that his knowledge and abilities were stunning. Because Wilson was regarded as a true talent to those who knew him, Fahey decided to bring him back to the West Coast. The two bonded intensely, relating to each other through their common unrequited romances, passions for musical obscurities, and family struggles. Fahey helped Wilson escape his unhappy East Coast life, something about which Fahey could empathize.

Fahey kept Wilson around as a roommate, paying him a tiny fee in exchange for access to his astounding transcription and musical notation skills. Wilson's unacknowledged contributions to Fahey's thesis would be invaluable. Though enthusiastic, there were limits to Fahey's scholarly abilities; he never learned to read, write, or transcribe music. Outsourcing this portion of the work left him plenty of time to expound on Patton's lyrical themes. He'd count how many references to death occurred in the musician's catalog, how many positive and negative references to women, and other sociological concerns in an almost pathological map of Patton's work. He and Wilson would sit up all night listening to old blues 78s and talking about their childhoods, commiserating on each other's sorrows and insecurities.

When they would socialize out of the house, the place to go for serious blues heads was Bob Hite's house in Topanga Canyon. Hite was a gregarious host; with a heavy frame and long hair, he earned the nickname "Bear." Musicians often came around the house for informal jam sessions. Hite was interested in putting together an electric jug band to play traditional tunes, and his large, commanding voice was perfect for leading a heavy band. Fahey invited Wilson, and Wilson and Hite hit it off. Another frequent regular was guitarist Henry Vestine, after he was kicked out of Frank Zappa's band for excessive drug use.

By late 1965, Hite, Wilson, and Vestine formed the core of the electric blues band Canned Heat. They cut their teeth on the L.A. club circuit, their set consisting of high-energy takes on classic blues songs. Onstage, Hite was the host of the band, just as he was the host of so many parties. Wilson bloomed as an expert guitarist, his exactitude envied by other blues players and his encyclopedic knowledge of country blues on full display. Vestine, in sharp juxtaposition to Wilson's traditional style, played wild guitar solos, increasingly psychedelic in technique, with howling feedback as a counterpoint. Focusing more on the postwar electric blues of artists like John Lee Hooker, Vestine played more sustained guitar runs and arpeggios against the rhythmic chug of Wilson's twelve-bar blues. This explosive combination of influences and styles eventually found international acclaim, but from the beginning, Canned Heat's common link was Fahey. In turn, he supported the band as individuals and encouraged them; though not part of the rock scene himself, he thought the band well-intentioned.

With interest in his work growing, Fahey began to play more concerts, getting booked in clubs and at folk festivals. Before then, his live experiences had been largely informal; back in Berkeley, he had played casually at parties or in smoke-filled clubs and coffeehouses on open mic nights. Increasingly, the pressure of being a professional entertainer in front of paid crowds began to weigh heavily on his nerves. As the demand for folk music surged, Fahey reluctantly forced himself into the role of showman. He was ill prepared to deal with the anxiety. Of all of the aspects of being a professional musician, live performance proved the most challenging for him. Stage fright became a powerful terror. When faced with performing in front of a paying audience, his aggressiveness came to the forefront as a defense mechanism. That trait soon turned into self-destruction.

To combat his fears he turned to alcohol as a crutch, often in copious amounts. His combination of insecurity and appetite was toxic. He infamously mixed bourbon into a large bottle of Coca-Cola and drank throughout his set, sometimes to the point of obliteration. As easy as it would be to keep silent, he often became vocal about his tensions. He sometimes became delirious on stage, ranting about politics or lecturing the crowd about how drugs, LSD in particular (although he had never tried it), were for the weak-minded. He seemed to challenge the mores of his new audience, if not out of spite, then in defense of his own fragility. In his drunken state, he strove to separate himself from the culture in which he found himself immersed.

His music drew the crowd in, but the man himself often became the greater spectacle. "I wouldn't describe him as a hard-core bigot or a right-winger, but he had grown up with old southern attitudes and understood them very well and sympathized with them," remembers Barry Hansen. "As he came to realize that many of his California listeners detested those attitudes, he would assume the role of a 'redneck' and bait his audience, using the n-word and all sorts of nasty language. I could be wrong, but I think he did that more for the sport of it, to get a rise out of people, and perhaps to make them realize that not everyone thought the same way as they did."

Fahey's natural tendency to be an instigator led to frequently uncomfortable performances during which he would openly goad the audience. Rather than assume the role of the victim, he lashed out. "I was playing an Al Capp role, calling them Communists and using the word 'nigger' and things, just to see if they really had any backbone," said Fahey. "Nobody ever said a word." Audiences were not there to be lectured about their lifestyles or politics, but Fahey's vehemence left few who challenged him.

He considered the left wing to be false and inauthentic around the issues of the working class, although he himself was a middle-class academic. He found the student Socialist and left-wing extremist movements to be obnoxious, noisy, and impotent. The power and force of his music matched his anticonformist viewpoints and left many listeners isolated in its wake. While some who came to his shows were advocates for mellowness or peace, Fahey attempted to channel darkness and dread through his music. Death continued to be a central theme of his work. His attempts to communicate openly with his "duped" audiences were poorly received. The hippies didn't appreciate the negativity Fahey brought to the table. David Cohen, guitarist for Country Joe & the Fish and a prominent musician on the Berkeley scene in his own right, recalls, "I thought Fahey was rather dark, and I didn't much care for musicians who drank on stage. I thought it was rude to the audience, which he certainly was, and contrived. Sometimes his pieces seemed to go on forever. He was a very difficult person to be friendly with, so after a couple of attempts, I stopped trying. Personally, I couldn't understand the fascination everyone had."

Sam Charters later infamously proclaimed Fahey to be the only artist that he knew whose sales went *down* following live shows. "I remember one night at a show in New York. He was sitting there with his bottle of whiskey in a paper bag, another bag that he spit into, and a two-quart bottle of Coke. It was a rather large crowd, and someone requested one of his songs. John said it was a hard song. He lit a cigarette and we watched him smoke the whole cigarette silent and looking off into space. He picked up the guitar and couldn't play it. It was too hard and he gave up."

His intense consumption escalated as his schedule expanded. He was a wreck. The audience became Fahey's victims—it being their fault, albeit unwittingly, that Fahey had to endure the torture of performance. He wrote one article called "Performance Is War" for a Canadian paper called the *Georgia Straight*, in which he fantasized about killing his audience then committing suicide onstage.

Put simply, he lacked the disposition of an entertainer. Fahey felt he functioned best as a scholar and composer, in isolated rooms, cutting tape or researching the minutiae of prewar blues 78s. This attitude had an obvious detrimental effect on Fahey's career as a musician. His reputation for drunken unprofessionalism and horrible stage interactions cost him access to a wider audience. While Fahey himself had little interest in the commercial world, those working at his label and management were quite invested in his success. Marketing a temperamental, antisocial guitar maverick was a difficult task, and he did nothing to make it any easier.

"He was very shy, which made him an awkward stage personality," says Denson. "He was known for things like smoking a cigarette, and between drags impaling the cigarette on the end of one of his guitar strings, or stopping mid-performance of a piece to take a long swig of Coca-Cola, then resuming the piece at the exact point at which he had stopped. I recall one traveler from Czechoslovakia who heard him perform in Berkeley and left saying, 'the man is just a clown.' John missed most of the potential he had for projects on a national or worldwide level because he could never adapt socially."

His social deviations were not merely combative, however. Having an audience gave the prankster in him a chance to subvert people's expectations. Ever the absurdist, Fahey often crossed the performer/audience divide. He would use his emerging cult status to his perceived advantage, however heavy handed. Once he got a small mimeograph machine and copied a note that read if he didn't find a girl who would marry him by the end of the night he was going to kill himself. He then placed these on the tables before he performed. Two girls came up to offer him their hand, but he didn't like them and declined.

Occasionally Fahey conjured sublime performances that exceeded the recorded versions in terms of performance and variation. One album, *The Great Santa Barbara Oil Slick*, was culled from two live performances in the 1960s and released posthumously in 2004. On it, a listener can find an easygoing Fahey performing a heartened take through his catalog. The audience laughs at his mild banter, and both performer and crowd seem happy. One can hear the appeal of Fahey's extended guitar work in a live setting: it is both hypnotic and all-encompassing. Never does it feel lacking in dynamics. On such good nights, Fahey successfully transformed the solo steel guitar into a concert instrument.

During the peak of the 1960s drug counterculture, audiences expected to be spellbound. Many ensured that this would be the case by coming high to the gigs. "I think he wanted people to listen, but he wanted them to overhear him playing to himself," says Charters. "They were there to notice. In Berkeley, when the audience was totally stoned, all they wanted was a mellifluous sound that was long. I did see him do whole theater concerts out there where the audience walked in stunned and walked out stunned."

While his career blossomed, his love life remained in disarray. All of his appetites were extreme in their fervor, but none seemed to invade his music like women. He had storybook ideas of true love that couldn't possibly match reality. When he fell for a girl, he fell hard—and he presented these various romances throughout his recorded work. He felt that deeply emotional circumstances prompted his best compositions. Fahey needed them as inspiration, giving them direct attention in his song titles and liner notes.

Among the most misguided of his romantic quests was the subject of one of his most beloved albums. Fahey met an attractive young lady named Linda Getchell, whom he quickly became infatuated with. Not since Pat Sullivan had a woman captivated him to such an extent. Getchell was taking summer classes at MIT when Fahey performed in Boston in 1965, but she also lived in Southern California. He proposed to her, but she turned him down, thinking the eccentric guitarist too much to handle. Still, she adored his music and the attention he gave her. She kept him at arm's length with promises of eventually being ready to return his affection. He wrote and recorded a song for her, boldly entitled "Beautiful Linda Getchell." Their relationship continued back on the West Coast while Fahey attended school and Getchell worked as a weather girl at a local television station in San Bernardino. She called a dejected Fahey and invited him to attend her birthday party there, a few hours south of Los Angeles. Fahey complained to her that the only reason she invited him was to play guitar for her friends and that she didn't care about his presence. He told her that all he wanted was a piece of cake and that he really didn't want to play any music. Getchell insisted that he need not worry.

Fahey and a few friends, including Al Wilson and Barry Hansen, drove down from Los Angeles to the party in Fahey's '55 Chevy. Getchell lived in the back of an older woman's house, which had a large backyard. When Getchell asked him to play a few songs for her guests—even though he had explicitly asked her not to—he became sullen. Feeling rejected and used, he reluctantly agreed. In the process he became toxically drunk. He stumbled off after a few short songs. His temper got the best of him. While most of the guests were in the backyard, Fahey and Getchell got into an intense argument in the kitchen. He accused her of leading him on, rejecting his advances and proposals. Furious and drunk, Fahey allegedly grabbed Getchell by the hair and slapped her in front of a few stupefied partygoers. "I remember he broke some of the landlady's china," recalls Hansen. "Linda was totally mortified. We beat a hasty retreat. John barfed out the rear passenger window; the stain stayed on the fender for weeks afterward. As far as I know, that was the end of beautiful Linda Getchell as part of John's life."

The incident provided the title for Fahey's fifth album, *The Great San Bernardino Birthday Party & Other Excursions*, released in 1966 on Takoma Records. The title track was inspired by Fahey's epic rejection at the hands of Getchell. (He later claimed the last six notes express "futility, a hopelessness and general existential despair complicated

by ontological absurdity," themes far from the political or romantic.) Compositionally it represented a departure from earlier material.
He incorporated bold new recording techniques that helped take the
music further from traditional roots. The pieces grew longer, with
experimental passages littered throughout. On the twenty-minute
title track, Fahey splices various takes together, creating unplayable
transitions through editing. A guitar will be in one tuning and then
a tape splice will have the guitar playing in an entirely different one
as if by magic. Additionally, the tape is run backwards, creating a
hallucinatory effect. The technique of musique concrète (a term referring to the combination of acoustic, electric, and ambient sounds)
adds a further dimension to Fahey's sound. Recalling the suite form
often found in classical music, Fahey was taking the acoustic guitar
into new contexts, eschewing the usual verse/chorus/verse structure
of most blues, folk, and country compositions. Many call this album
psychedelic, as its sound contains elements not in any other record
found under folk in the record store. The music's extended melodic
passages often created hypnotic, repetitive patterns conducive to the
effects of hallucinogens.

Another musical anomaly of the record is the duet between Fahey
and former roommate Al Wilson, who guests on the song "Sail Away
Ladies" playing the vina, a South Indian instrument that predates
the sitar. The track was the most mystical, Eastern-sounding song in
Fahey's catalog to date, and became a favorite with taste-making UK
DJ John Peel, who was largely responsible for cultivating Fahey's audience in Europe. Wilson learned the instrument in two days, making
the recording on that second day of the pair's time in Boston. The song
contains edited sections of an hour-plus session and combines blues
with raga in a hypnotic swirl. This vivid approach was uncharted territory for the two blues fanatics.

Despite the innovations, lingering traces of the past remain on the record. Anthony Lee makes his only Fahey-accompanied performance, playing organ on the standard "Will the Circle Be Unbroken." The track dated back to St. Michael's in May 1962 and was culled from Fahey's personal archive of recordings. Fahey and Lee's version has a more Pentecostal feel than most, because of the church organ. The song serves as a hymnal intermission for the album. Old friend Nancy McLean also makes an appearance, on a flute duet with Fahey on "900 Miles," which was recorded in the same St. Michael's era. The traditional songs mix with the more experimental techniques to make a hodgepodge collection of tracks.

He may have traveled west, but the ghosts of Takoma Park still roamed the highways of Fahey's mind, as the hymns recorded at the church there attest. Fahey appreciated religion and its relationship with death, the concepts of salvation and freedom from bondage. By no means is Fahey proselytizing on the record; rather, he is exploring the language of the spiritual, a counterpoint to the hedonistic blues that also fascinated him.

The fragmentation of sounds highlights the psychedelic feel of *The Great San Bernardino Birthday Party*. One moment the listener is in Maryland, another California, transported through different years with no real explanation or transition. Regardless of intent, it was the right record for an audience beginning to experiment with abstract sounds. Those who tuned in were finding music that fit a more altered way of thinking.

The audience is also introduced to a new persona in the Fahey universe, the character of Knott's Berry Farm Molly. Molly was a young woman who lived out by the amusement park Knott's Berry Farm. Her courtship with Fahey was more reciprocal than his one-sided obsession with Getchell, although ultimately just as fleeting.

The track "Knott's Berry Farm Molly" features a haunting finger-picked melody played in standard tuning in the keys of C and D. Then, using multiple recording tracks, Fahey incorporates backwards looping. Everything turns around in a swirl of warped, stretched guitar sounds, as if the tape were being manually turned in the other direction against its will. In fact, Fahey recorded a version of "Canned Heat Blues" by Tommy Johnson and recorded it backwards to achieve the desired effect, putting it together alone in his house with a tape recorder. Fahey got the idea from the Beatles' "Rain," as Molly was a big Beatles fan.

Perhaps the theme for this record lies in the dichotomy of Linda Getchell and Molly, and what they represented. There was the unattainable beauty Linda and the sympathetic and sweet Molly. Molly seemed to patch the wound of Linda and provide a counterbalance. *The Great San Bernardino Birthday Party* brings Fahey closer than ever to telling the actual stories of his romantic pratfalls, however skewed they might seem.

By the time the album was released, Molly was long gone. Fahey claimed she ended the relationship because she wanted a Jewish husband and she didn't believe he'd convert for her. He appreciated her genuine affection and dedication to him, but ultimately he wanted something more dynamic. Still, he thought about marriage and settling down. He soon found a partner who had all the things he was looking for.

Jan Lebow first became acquainted with Fahey at UCLA. A Jewish girl from a self-described pinko liberal California family, Lebow came from a far different background than the twenty-seven-year-old Fahey. A pretty brunette undergrad studying zoology, she ended up interning one day a week in the graduate folklore department, where Fahey held court. He had already established a reputation around campus as an underground hero. She had seen him play and knew him as a musician of considerable appeal, and she played acoustic guitar as well. One day while hanging around school, they were introduced. He asked her to be his date for a concert he was performing at UCSB and took her along to Santa Barbara. The two began a romance, and it wasn't long before he proposed. Lebow seemed to possess the sensitivity needed to appreciate his artistic temperament, but she also encouraged healthy lifestyle choices and better living. "He understood that he wasn't really good at the day-to-day stuff and he needed someone to take care of him. That was me for a while," admits Jan. Keeping him in line was no small feat.

To Jan, the attraction was based not only on his fiery musicality but the thoughtful, gentle side that he rarely showed anyone outside his closest friends. "Underneath the bravado and the outrageousness he was really pathologically shy. He was a fascinating man, very bright, very philosophical. He was eccentric, he was unusual, but he was together," she recalls. In Lebow, he had found someone who complemented him, and his desperation eased. A health food expert, she cooked for him and got him to quit his massive Coca-Cola intake. There were other habits that proved more difficult to break. "Even then he always had problems sleeping, so he'd be up late at night and play and then he'd sleep most of the day," she recalls. "I'm an early person and he was a night owl and he always said he had trouble sleeping, so he took downers at night and uppers during the day and that was his cycle. He smoked like a fiend." Despite their differences, the couple found enough common ground, and Fahey tried to adjust to the structure of a traditional relationship.

VOICE OF THE TURTLE

"Turtles are my favorite animals. Everybody runs over them on the highways and that's why I want to kill everybody. That's one reason I want to kill everybody."

—John Fahey, interview, 1970

In 1966, Denson began consolidating his many ventures. Under the banner Joyful Wisdom Enterprises he managed Takoma Records, along with artists Fahey, Robbie Bǎsho, and the far more successful Country Joe & the Fish. His headquarters occupied the second floor of a building on Adeline Street at Ashby Street in Berkeley. The building, then in a rough industrial neighborhood, had six rooms with offices for the small staff, a rehearsal space for Country Joe & the Fish, and two rooms where Denson and others lived periodically. The accommodations were far from luxurious but suited their purposes.

Denson hired Tom Weller as art director, to give Takoma Records a modern overhaul. Weller had designed most of the concert posters for shows at Berkeley's famous folk club the Jabberwock, so he fit the natural aesthetic for Takoma in its new home. Weller's signature style echoed the growing radicalism of the hippie movement, in keeping with the vibrant, colorful visuals of the era. Unlike the stodgy, drab folk records of the time, his bold designs attracted younger, hip listeners and helped push the label to the next level in terms of visibility. The album art for Takoma became far more psychedelic and ornate, in line with the poster art explosion. Weller created iconography that would define the Fahey legacy for decades to come, though Fahey himself was almost completely uninvolved. "I never got any input from Fahey, nor any feedback," recalls Weller. "I had carte blanche on the Takoma covers and I just did what I wanted. Except one time he stuck his head in the door of the studio, said, 'Don't ever make anything that puke green color again,' and left."

In the two-year span from 1967 to 1968, Fahey released five full-length albums: *Days Have Gone By*, *Requia*, *The Voice of the Turtle*, *The Yellow Princess*, and *The New Possibility*. In addition, Takoma repackaged Fahey's back catalog with new artwork. In addition to new, more eye-catching cover designs, Fahey rerecorded his first two albums in stereo (the initial pressings were in the by-then-outdated mono format). As the lead force of the label, Fahey was well represented in his label's catalog and he was pleased to have his records in print to meet the growing demand for his music.

Though updated for the times, the content of Fahey's music was still death-obsessed. The grinning skeletons on the reissue of Fahey's third album, *Dance of Death* (1965), echo the music's darker themes and appealed to a new audience of 1960s music fans searching for new sounds. The images were adapted from a book of medieval woodcuts depicting, yes, the dance of death. The harmony in the artwork of the recently reissued albums gave Fahey's catalog a sense of continuity. They were now subtitled with volume numbers (volume 1, volume 2, and so on), and together stood as the saga of Fahey in installments. Every record became a chapter in an ongoing narrative.

The fact that he chose to rerecord the music of his first two albums in their entirety was evidence not only of his increased prowess on the guitar but also of his constant insecurity. He couldn't let go of these early pieces and revisited them constantly. While the redone versions sound far better in performance and fidelity, something of the charm and sloppy feel of the initial material remains. Takoma also kept the original versions of the first two Fahey albums in print, as *The Early Sessions*, volumes 1 and 2, for the purists, obsessives, and simply curious.

Taken together, Fahey's first ten albums contain all of the recordings and compositions he had been working on since he began playing guitar. Most of his Takoma releases were put together from different recording sessions and eras, like a patchwork, and they vary in style and fidelity. As Fahey's appeal continued to grow, Takoma began releasing his work in a flurry.

In early 1967, Takoma also released a compilation album entitled *Contemporary Guitar*, featuring contributions from Fahey, Băsho, Bukka White, Max Ochs, and Harry Taussig. Here, the label's aesthetic was clearly presented: instrumental guitar composition. From blues to raga to folk, the album made a strong case for the Takoma label's aesthetic, while showcasing the myriad influences and variations under its umbrella. The Weller-designed artwork of the first pressing of the compilation was boldly psychedelic, echoing the iconography of the Fillmore Theater posters of the day and using the surrealistically illustrated typography typically associated with hallucinogens. Indeed, there was nothing traditional about how this record looked or sounded. And the instrumental template offered limitless possibilities for guitar players and solo musicians.

While Takoma was a fine outlet for Fahey's home-recorded experiments, he yearned for the resources to attempt grander statements.

He still wanted to record for larger labels, with which he could find a budget to actualize his more ambitious and elaborate musical concepts. The next step in his career would bring Fahey into the professional music industry in a whole new way, complete with publicity, marketing, and distribution, the likes of which Takoma had never seen. As audiences began to change, larger companies would become increasingly interested in underground music.

Outside of Fahey's self-created, insular universe, folk music had become a pop phenomenon. Acts like Peter, Paul and Mary and the Mamas and the Papas were selling records by the millions. Record labels were racing to snatch up new folk acts. Bob Dylan had set the template for folk singer as superstar and made a fortune in sales for Columbia Records.

Dylan's female counterpart in the 1960s antiwar movement was Joan Baez, whose ascent took struggling independent Vanguard Records to major-label heights. Started in 1950 by brothers Maynard and Seymour Solomon, Vanguard established itself as a vehicle for mostly classical music, issuing works by Charles Ives, Prokofiev, and Mozart among many others. By the early 1960s the label set its sights on the emerging folk sounds coming from the West Coast. As the symbolic home to a new wave of political dissent, Berkeley had given birth to the student protest movement, and the music scene there was thriving. Soon enough, A&R men from the major labels came to check out the scene.

Vanguard hired Sam Charters as a talent scout. Having just recorded Buddy Guy, Otis Rush, and Junior Wells among others for the Prestige label, he had already worked with many guitar legends. Vanguard had their eyes on a number of big acts, Country Joe & the Fish among their top priorities. Charters successfully signed them and produced their first three albums. Released in 1967, the band's second, *I-Feel-Like-I'm-Fixin'-to-Die,* became Vanguard's biggest hit since Baez.

While in California, Charters was determined to check up on Fahey, having remembered him from their earlier correspondence. He had kept his copy of the original *Blind Joe Death* album and set off to find the man behind it. Although Charters had rejected Fahey's debut, he changed his mind upon hearing his second album in 1964 and had since become an advocate of Fahey's work. He decided to drop by UCLA on a trip to Los Angeles to meet Fahey in person. He showed up early to one of Fahey's classes and sat in the back of the room as the students arrived. "John came in wearing a turtleneck, looking very much like a graduate student, and walked immediately to the blackboard; I was watching him, he didn't look my way," remembers Charters. "The teacher said 'John, there's someone here who wants to meet you,' and without turning around he said, 'Hi, Sam.'"

The two quickly became friends. Fahey came to realize firsthand the difficulties of recording old bluesmen and had a newfound appreciation for Charters's work in that field. Charters, in turn, felt Fahey had progressed as a musician enough to record for a bigger company. Charters worked to sign Fahey to Vanguard, despite the guitarist's perceived lack of commercial appeal. Vanguard had prior cult success with Sandy Bull, a contemporary of Fahey and an improvisational guitarist with stronger jazz leanings and eclectic skill. However, by 1966, Bull had become so addicted to heroin that he was unable to write new material. In effect, Vanguard saw Fahey as filling Bull's shoes as the label's acoustic guitar maverick.

Fahey's dream was for Vanguard to let him make a record with an orchestra. He had great respect for the label's classical line, which made up half the label's catalog. He asked Charters if he could have his record released on the label's classical imprint, but the request went unheeded as the label saw him as a contemporary folk artist.

Still, it was a great step forward to work with a big New York record company with a studio budget. Charters was attached to produce the project. For the first time Fahey had the opportunity to connect with a larger audience. And the album he submitted to Charters would be among his most unusual and nontraditional recording to date.

One clear aspect of Fahey's intent was the incorporation of modern classical ideas and found sounds into traditional melodic American guitar forms. While several of his albums featured elements of collage and edits of field recordings mixed in, no greater was this approach heard than on Fahey's 1967 Vanguard Records debut, *Requia*. The record, along its course, samples Charles Ives, obscure brass band and string quartet recordings, Charley Patton, Adolf Hitler speeches, military sounds, field recordings of bridges, and other found sound objects to form a pastiche. Throughout, Fahey incorporates ambient recordings of nature and splices field recordings into the music. Bringing together such disparate elements, the collages show their seams, and often are at odds with Fahey's own tempered playing. The most experimental aspect is his use of alternate tunings, which he describes in his liner notes as a freeing experience. The source materials here work as additional narrative to Fahey's pristinely rudimentary melodies, creating a musical template as grandiose as, and often more extreme than, any "art rock" record of its time period.

The album opens conservatively enough with a tribute to the then–recently departed Mississippi John Hurt. The central theme of the track is Patton's version of "Jesus Is a Dying Bed Maker." However, it is not the only Patton reference found on *Requia*.

The second side is where things turn experimental, with a four-part suite entitled "Requiem for Molly," a tribute to his ex-girlfriend Molly. The recently unearthed Patton record "Circle Round the Moon" was edited and used in shards in a bizarre psychedelic duet of spliced tape with Fahey playing a haunting fingerpicked melody underneath. Using harsh cuts of Patton singing and playing interspersed, like the sound of paper being ripped loudly over Fahey's playing, the piece sounded unlike anything else. Later on, in "Requiem for Molly (Part 4)," in juxtaposition to the obscure Patton reference, Fahey echoes the melody of "California Dreamin'" by the Mamas and the Papas. Again, Fahey throws listeners' expectations a curveball; he was not above the pleasure of a popular melody.

The album, like all Fahey albums to this point, ends with a spiritual: the hymn "Fight On Christians, Fight On," perhaps washing away the sins of his experimentalism with a taste of the traditional.

Requia's audio collages and panning techniques were jarring, yet certainly effective as a piece of psychedelia, a movement then in full bloom. The music's repetitive foundation—long, melodic stretches of open-tuned notes—made for a resplendent soundtrack to the hallucinations of LSD. Fahey's intentions were not to soundtrack a good time. Instead, he was celebrating a descent into madness and an indulgence with death, each track a reminder of mortality. A magazine advertisement for the album features a picture of a suit-clad Fahey sitting in front of a large tombstone with his name and the album details engraved on it. It's not hard to see why Fahey didn't connect with the hippie zeitgeist of the time; the morbid scene expressed the opposite of peace and love.

Despite the incredibly difficult content of *Requia*, Fahey knew that Vanguard would give him access to a wider audience. Certainly no other record being marketed and sold in the folk sections at retailers contained such confrontational radicalism and harsh audio content. Although the A-side seemed appropriate, the B-side, with its boldly experimental sounds, belonged more with the modern avant-garde of John Cage or Morton Subotnik than the formalism of songwriters like Pete Seeger. But records need to sit *somewhere* on the shelves, and the record was still marketed as an acoustic guitar album.

In the liner notes, Fahey largely abandons the abstract farce of his other albums and adopts a more reverent tone, looking back to his earliest inclinations as a musician.

> Since 1948, after seeing the movie, *The Thief of Bagdad* I com-posed cerebral symphonies every day. It was a pleasant pastime. But suddenly in 1953 I needed a full orchestra at my command— and me playing every instrument in that impossible ensemble (Impossible! It would have had to include a full Western High-Art orchestra, bagpipes, Rahet Ek Lek, Saron, Sarangi, Gender and numerous other instruments). Furthermore, there was no time to study composition, conducting etc. Besides I was too young. I needed it then, immediately, to drown out with music, the new disturbing sounds I heard emanating for my own fear and ignorance of the ways of men and women; from the contempt I felt for the fact that I had no driver's license; and so far of course I had to drown out the sound of the traffic on the road east. Now I have learned to drive quite well, have a license, and I see that I have learned the ways of men and women just as well, but unfortunately a little too late. So in celebration of time wasted I continue to play the guitar.

Fahey had assembled the various sounds he wanted to collage, and then the album was largely arranged by producer Sam Charters. Their often difficult relationship extended into the recording process. "This was the frustration for him, that he wasn't the one cutting the tape. It was the first time when he had to sit down with a studio engineer," says Charters. "John would drink and work alone at night. He was losing control. He was gaining more opportunity, better studio, better sound, all these pluses, but *Requia* was not a happy album. When we finished I thought it was really depressing, but I respected John so much as an artist."

Charters had to contend with an unresponsive artist in Fahey, but he knew what he was getting into. "I did a rough mix of it and I had a lot of fun doing it. If you listen to it on a good stereo you can hear the train pan around and around," says Charters. "I did an editing of everything and did the whole album and sent it to John and then nothing. Months went by and he couldn't finish the damn thing. He had never released anything without months of fiddling with it, and I told him it was done. I asked him over and over what he wanted me to do—phone calls, letters—and just nothing but procrastination. He'd taken a step beyond where he knew. It wasn't hostility, but he just wasn't used to telling someone else how to work with his own materials." This shift in process alienated Fahey. Not being in control, and not trusting Charters, left him deadlocked.

On the album jacket, a stoic-looking Fahey sits with his hands on his knees, staring into the camera. His clean white shirt is tucked into a gray suit; he wears a modest blue tie. His hair short, his face clean-shaven, he presents himself in stark contrast to the hedonism of the left-wing movement that was running wild.

Vanguard didn't expect much in terms of sales from the record. The label had no illusions about him being Joan Baez, Buffy Sainte-Marie, or Country Joe & the Fish, the label's breadwinners at the time. "He was a prestige artist, the kind of artist we believed in," adds Charters. "There had been, at the beginning, antagonism, and he respected what I did recording the blues, but he did not like the fact that I was working with the Fish because they were a commercial band. Finally we reached a deadline when the first year we had was up, so I released it—and John was very, very angry. I found out that this was his pattern—he did this to Ed Denson—but I was culpable."

Upon the album's release in 1967, Fahey stated bluntly, "*Requia* stinks. I was drunk during the recording sessions and they put the splices in the wrong places. Don't buy it. It's bad news." He painted himself as the classic temperamental artist, constantly displeased; his statements seemed a blatant insult to the label and producer who took a chance on him. The response to the album was solid but commercially unspectacular. The general public was more interested in electric rock music than a multigenre approach to instrumental music. "Vanguard needed a megahit," says Charters. "They didn't need to sell thirty, forty thousand. The first Country Joe & the Fish record sold 850,000 in the first couple of months."

Fahey remained hesitant about careerism, in any respect. "What I have is this, and it is very important," he said. "I have a small little niche carved out here where I play guitar for people once in a great while. I make just enough money to get by and have a little left over. And that's all I want to do. For me, to work any harder than that would be unethical and greedy." Ultimately, those in his circle were less idealistic; they were far too busy with more pressing financial concerns. Charters, Denson, and even Al Wilson were all riding the rush of the 1960s rock 'n' roll commercial success as both Country Joe & the Fish and Canned Heat gained national attention.

In the midst of it all, John Fahey and Jan Lebow got married in a small ceremony in California on June 24, 1967. "We got married here but we went back east to have a private ceremony with his priest," says Jan. "No family, just the two of us and the priest. The only one of his family that came was his grandfather's brother, who was a really nice man."

Later that summer, the newlyweds went canvassing for records, driving through the South. Fahey showed Jan the ropes of the collector trade. She had never traveled the region, and she saw the trip as an adventure. "We were young and it was fun," Jan remembers. "We went to some general store in the South and they had a wind-up portable Victrola and they still had needles for them. He got a box of needles, and we would go door to door in these ancient black neighborhoods that they still called 'the quarters,' for slave quarters, and people would have a few records. We would go and we'd fill up the entire backseat of the station wagon and he would drive and I would play them on the Victrola. I'd have it on my lap. So I'd play them, and if he liked [the record] he would put it in the backseat; if he didn't, it would go sailing out the window." They would end up making around $1,000 after selling the bulk to private collectors upon their return, something they would do after each trip. Not a bad haul for a young couple in love.

During this time, Fahey completed his thesis on Patton, a largely theoretical and obsessive take on the artist's known recordings. His findings were well received by the academic and blues scholar communities and helped cement his reputation as an authority in his field, far beyond the average fan. Seen as a formidable, scholarly work, simply titled *Charley Patton*, the 112-page book was eventually published, in England by Studio Vista in November 1970, in a limited run as part of a series of chapbooks. The book became a seminal volume among blues fanatics.

Having completed his master's and newly contented in his personal life, Fahey focused on his musical activities with renewed vigor, stimulated by new opportunities for his art and his hopes for finding an audience that understood it. His visits to Berkeley and the Takoma offices became less frequent. Things in Berkeley were beginning to become far more commercial. The counterculture attracted attention around the world and money started to enter the scene. Yet Fahey remained outside, while his label partner Denson was flooded with new responsibilities as manager of Country Joe & the Fish.

Although Fahey became the public face of the label, much of what it became known for can be attributed to Denson's vision and savvy. Fahey often criticized him for the decisions that he made in regards to marketing or design, and felt any success he had was innately due to his own efforts as a musician. But with Takoma's roster growing, Fahey could no longer claim the label as his own, and conflicts of interest began to emerge. Denson wanted Takoma to be a commercial success, while Fahey was more preoccupied by his own recordings and touring. "As far as commerciality, I don't think John ever once made a single concession," says Charters. "Ed did. He was always pushing and believed totally in John as an artist. John demanded or expected a great deal of attention, but he also didn't want your attention. It was so damn complicated."

In the era of free-spirited abandon and love, Fahey seemed staunchly prudish by comparison, set adrift among the counterculture by virtue of his psychedelic album covers and spellbinding music. Another notable connection was his collaboration with Texas-based psychedelic band the Red Crayola—later the Red Krayola. The band, led by guitarist Mayo Thompson, was an improvisation-based trio. In live settings, they often abandoned form entirely and largely made up their performances on the spot. Fahey found their approach freeing, and it appealed to his absurdist sense of humor. He performed live with the band in Los Angeles on July 3, 1967—just a week after his wedding. Their set retained little semblance of rock music, instead exploring the inaccessible. Having gotten along well, the band and Fahey decided to book studio time to record an entire collaborative album for the Red Crayola's label at the time, International Artists.

Label head Lelan Rogers rejected the results, and the tapes were never heard again. This shelved collaboration was an anomaly; Fahey remained a solo act, preferring to work on his own terms.

He then turned back to Takoma Records to create one of his most ambitious works. *The Voice of the Turtle* offers a more in-depth look at the artist than any in his catalog. The album exists as a world unto itself, so rich with symbolism that it functions more as semifictional autobiography than an album.

Here Fahey introduces his audience for the first time to the turtle, a recurring presence throughout his life. He considered himself an amateur expert on turtles and kept many as pets around his house, sometimes more than a dozen. If he saw a turtle crossing a highway he would stop, get out of his car, and bring it to the other side of the road so it wouldn't be harmed. Once when he and Jan were visiting a local pet store, Fahey became appalled at the conditions in which the turtles were kept. He decided to buy all thirteen turtles they had in the store, despite having no idea what to do with them. Once they rescued the creatures from their cages, Fahey had to keep them all in his bathtub. Whenever he or Jan wanted to take a shower they had to remove the turtles and then scrub the tub clean from turtle dung. They kept it up for a few weeks, but then even Fahey had to concede that they had to go. Though he didn't have the means, he would prefer to have lived with as many as he could.

In terms of artwork and layout, *The Voice of the Turtle* is Fahey's most sprawling and elaborate album, with a twelve-page insert that includes extensive pictures and liner notes. The package reads like a museum exhibit whose narration spirals into the absurd. "He didn't say anything about the cover, but for that insert of his, um, deranged ranting, he brought over all the materials and told me exactly what he wanted," remembers cover designer Tom Weller, "so I precisely followed what he said." The booklet, also titled "The Fahey Picture Album," is littered with images of people and places, notably Fahey's ex-girlfriends. Knott's Berry Farm Molly, Linda Getchell of the *Great San Bernardino Birthday Party*, and Pat Sullivan (dubbed Evil Devil Woman below her picture) are all seen for the first time. He had written songs featuring the real women in his life, and they had also become recurring characters in his liner notes—but now his audience could see them vividly for the first time. None of the women were asked permission—or even informed that their pictures would adorn his records.

It was a first for a record of any kind, and a communication to the audience that was personal but also obscure, as the public had little idea who these people were. Yet to those who knew him, it was a diary. "I'm not aware of any other musician who put out anything remotely resembling the presentation of *The Voice of the Turtle* before that came out," says Barry Hansen. "He had these surrealistic ideas running around in his brain starting at a very early age, probably before he began recording. When people started asking him why the heck he named one of his instrumental pieces 'Stomping Around on the Pennsylvania-Alabama Border' [*sic*] he began to think that some of his followers might be interested in some of those thought processes, and eventually began writing them down. I had no idea that he was using a snapshot of me [for the insert of *The Voice of the Turtle*] until he handed me a finished copy."

In addition to his lovers, he included images of his friends and relatives, and even Takoma Park. Characters like Chester C. Petranick (the real-life inspiration for Fahey's pseudonym), his grandparents, and shots of guest musicians littered the pages. Other images included blues legend Son House's birthplace, the Takoma Park Funeral Home, and Barry Hansen holding a rare Jelly Roll Morton record during a canvassing trip. The back cover showed a photo of Fahey as a seventeen-year-old, exhibiting a public distance and an intense stare, his hair slicked back in a classic 1950s greaser pompadour.

The overall effect was of an elaborately narrated photo album. Everyone became a part of his universe, like constellations, laid out in a virtual confessional art exhibit. "Notes, in those days, were often intended to convince people to buy a record, but that doesn't seem to be the case here," adds Hansen. "I think that in the final analysis he was writing for himself . . . using writing to sort out all the things that obsessed him, writing to help mitigate the ways those things disturbed, even tormented him. Eventually, of course, his writing became an end unto itself, still related to his music but not attempting to explain any particular pieces."

Released on Takoma in 1968, *The Voice of the Turtle* is a musical collage as well as a visual one. In his most elaborate prank, Fahey released two different albums with the exact same cover, booklet, and track titles—but with completely different recordings. Each pressing of the record contained a different sequence and music. It was yet another vexing display of Fahey's absurd humor. These alternate versions of the same album remain the most confusing part of his discography, since they were indistinguishable to the record-buying public save by the color of the center label.

Fahey created an audio patchwork that properly mirrored the timeline of the notes, using recordings from throughout his personal archive. He starts the album with the traditional "Bottleneck Blues," a 1927 performance by Weaver & Beasley, with which Fahey plays along on the record—another prank on the listener. The track is credited to John Fahey and Blind Joe Death. In the process, Fahey literally plays on top of his favorite records and uses them as his own in an attempt to place himself into his beloved blues history.

After "Bottleneck," the album shifts to the more modern, psychedelic ragas of the oft-reprised Fahey composition "A Raga Called Pat."
Part 3 ends the A-side, and part 4 begins the B-side. These two tracks
offer a surreal counterpoint to traditional, Tin Pan Alley nostalgia
of earlier tracks including "Bean Vine Blues." After "Pat," a flurry of
guests appear on the record. Most notable are the performances (again
from Fahey's personal archive) featuring Nancy McLean on flute.

Also included are two pieces recorded on a 1966 canvassing trip
with Hansen. The pair went to Oklahoma, northeast Texas, Arkansas,
and northern Louisiana. The official reason for the trip was to record
two old-time fiddlers, Hubert Thomas and Virgil Willis Johnston.
Arrangements for the visits had been made in advance, and they spent
an afternoon/early evening with each fiddler. Hansen ran the UCLA
Folklore Department's AMPEX tape deck while Fahey supervised the
sessions, sometimes accompanying the fiddlers on guitar. The album
concludes with one such collaboration, the spiritual "Lonesome Valley." Ending with a spiritual, he echoes an old Nashville tradition of
praising the Lord to wash away the secular damage of earlier tracks—
a typical end to a Fahey record. Fahey also uses the idea of ending
with a spiritual as a social critique, attacking in his liner notes those
who he feels are insincere in their musical presentation.

Fahey sought the feelings they stirred, not the stylistic conventions, of those old blues records. He rarely played them in those
days; he was writing his own music, assured of his vision. In his liner
notes, under the guise of a narrator Fahey evaluates his own art: "The
recordings which comprise this record comprise a well defined yet
non-directive channel of Mr. Fahey's roots and the progression of his
music for the casual listener to be entertained thereby, the inquisitive
listener thus may have his curiosity satisfied and the casual listener
may, in the same manner, as it were be entertained," he said in his

best faux-scholar voice. Fahey continues, "The former is exactly the point of this record: A history, chronicle and documentary recording—all in one—of Mr. Fahey's musical creations, and of what is, to the scholar, or the inquisitor of more significance, Mr. Fahey's musical influences which led to his creations." In doing so, he explicitly shows his influences as musical and biographical. Further, the women in his life are given an equal influence to the musicians and scholars whose work he so greatly admired.

If one can feel the haze of the Delta while hearing Son House then certainly the silhouettes of the Adelphi Rolling Grist Mill and the presence of Blind Joe Death can be felt in the recorded work of John Fahey. The pieces form a view of Fahey from all angles—the professional, the myth, the collector, the romantic, the scholar—and form the sum total of his early American experience. The result sounds almost like a conversation the artist is having with himself, rearranging and editing the details of his life. All the while, the audience is privy to this process, and its voyeuristic indulgence becomes a justification for Fahey's self-obsessions. After all, Fahey himself fantasized about his work being viewed with the same level of devotion as that of his idols.

"He was unassailably convinced of his importance," says Sam Charters. "As for mythology, didn't he do for himself what he did for Charley Patton? That was his blueprint. He became a legendary figure just like Patton was. When John did the Patton book we didn't know very much about him. It was largely conjecture, a musical interpretation in a way. So yes, I think this was the working template for what John was doing. It's easy to fall into. It's a kind of presentation that you understand has value and has a methodology. So he did his own version of a methodology, a working musicologist, and he did it on himself while creating the music at the same time. You get a wonderful parallel universe, of him creating the document while documenting its creation at the same time."

Yet *The Voice of the Turtle* was a financial disaster. The bulky packaging cost 15 cents more per unit to manufacture than the wholesale price at which the company sold it, so they lost money on every copy sold. According to Fahey, no one at Takoma figured this out until a year after its release.

In the meantime, despite Fahey's frustrations with Vanguard and the outcome of *Requia*, he moved forward with another ambitious creation for the label. It would ultimately become one of his most beloved and recognized achievements. In stark contrast to the brooding and difficult *Requia*, *The Yellow Princess* offered the opposite in tonality and approach.

In February 1968, Fahey simply asked Barry Hansen if he would help produce his next album, and Hansen quickly agreed. Charters, busy with various other projects, gladly handed over the studio reins to Hansen, whom he trusted implicitly. "With *Yellow Princess*, John talked about working with bands, so I told him I would stay in New York and he could work with Barry—and Barry was great," says Charters. "John said he wanted a tape recorder to record the sound of the bridge on his way back to California so I bought him a tape recorder. John admired Barry's record collection, which was absolutely staggering. I knew Barry was sympathetic musically and I trusted what he would do, and I absolutely love the album. I think it's a masterpiece."

The crisp, robust sound of the album showed that recording in a studio as opposed to his home recording techniques had benefitted *Yellow Princess*. Hansen's easy temperament and vast musical knowledge enhanced his job as producer. And Fahey had hit a stride in his increasing proficiency on guitar. Fahey's compositions feel fully thought out, and his picking is perfectly executed.

The title track, which begins the album, contains both a confidence and a peace not often found on Fahey's songs. Its melodic conclusion is technically dazzling, and notably bright for the oft-gloomy Fahey. Its title alludes to the name of a clipper ship that he saw in 1953 in Virginia. In fact, the piece was originally started in 1954, then eventually completed in 1966 in Bastrop, Louisiana, according to the album's notes.

Hansen recalls the solo recording for the sessions as being effortless. "The title song was the first song recorded, and John nailed it in one take. The other solo guitar pieces came off very easily as well. John and I had previously spent several evenings in L.A. going over the material and picking the best pieces. That process was very amicable."

"Lion," a spirited tribute to his recently departed cat of the same name, is the album's third track, meditative but hardly morose. It is more of a playful celebration of meandering melody lines than a sentimental ballad. This is followed immediately by Fahey's only political ode, "March for Martin Luther King," of which he asks in the notes, "Why didn't we all? Maybe some of us will now; maybe it's too late." The track includes a military-style drum tapping; eventually a full backing band comes in behind him, with organ, bass, and drum. Fahey rounds out the side with an audio collage of field recordings, presumably of the bridge of its title: "The Singing Bridge of Memphis, Tennessee." (Vanguard would release "March"/"Singing" as a seven-inch promo for the album.)

The second side begins dramatically, with the soaring "Dance of the Inhabitants of the Invisible City of Bladensburg," which transforms into a full-blown blues-rock outro. On it, he employs a full backing band made up of members of the band Spirit, whom Hansen called on for the sessions. Hansen recalls, "That session was star-crossed, because Robert Kennedy was shot the night before, and everyone was disturbed and distracted on account of that. It was my idea to produce an electric version of 'Dance of the Inhabitants . . .' and John was not thrilled with the idea but agreed to give it a go. It was of course his first experience with anything resembling electric rock music" (apart from his experience with the Red Crayola). "He groused and grumbled all the way but gave it his best shot." The addition of these band members help to make *The Yellow Princess* accessible, while still unyielding in artistic vision, since the new techniques remain sparse.

The album features classic Fahey solo performances as well, such as "Charles A. Lee: In Memoriam," a track dedicated to the memory of Anthony Lee's father. He wrote in a section of the notes, "Noted icthyologist [*sic*] who accidentally saved the lives of thousands of people through his research. Father of my best and oldest friend, Flea. C.A.L. was murdered in Brazil in 1966. I hardly knew him but I knew enough." The album ends with the epic "Commemorative Transfiguration and Communion at Magruder Park." The title alludes to a magical fantasy experience—the coming of his fictional childhood messiah, the Great Koonaklaster—about which he would later write at great length.

The album cover is a colorful abstract representation of the album notes, with drawings of Fahey playing guitar, the mast of the clipper ship towering in the foreground, a turtle blending into the background. On the back is a black-and-white photo of Fahey staring off into the distance, his torso contrasting with a cloudy skyline, the wind blowing his hair. "I did not go east," Fahey wrote in the liner notes. "I took the wrong passage. Still, I thought, maybe I had gotten somewhere. Maybe I did. Who knows? But I am reminded of a quote from Whitman, which seems appropriate. '. . . Where is what I started for so long ago? And why is it yet unfound?'"

His notes for the album are direct and noticeably avoid his trademark obfuscation, instead featuring a transcendental theme mixed with a sincere self-reflection. However, the writing moves between lucidity and dreamlike prose. For the first time, he seems to be speaking in his own voice, not that of the faux scholar or the hidden narrator of dubious credibility. Fahey, like his blues heroes, had come to a crossroads. Revealing his true self to his audience—and to himself—marked a new level of confidence for the artist as a writer.

The Yellow Princess remains a perfect idealized interaction between Fahey and the 1960s counterculture. With hints of rock and expanded musical vocabulary, the album teems with new ideas. Nowhere can themes of death or misplaced anxieties be found. Marketed to a wide audience, the album offered a perfect entry into Fahey's music. The album sold reasonably well: around fifty thousand copies at the time of its release. For many, it served as a gentle introduction to the oftdour world of John Fahey. Even the title spoke more relevantly to the times than the death odes and personal grudges of Fahey albums past. For once, a disposition of possibility and hope seemed to shine through the author's impenetrable, detached visage.

While Charters was off with the Fish, Fahey got involved professionally with Vanguard's new West Coast A&R man and producer Denny Bruce, a onetime drummer for Frank Zappa's Mothers of Invention. Bruce had gone on to work with artists like Tina Turner, Magic Sam, and Buffy Sainte-Marie in various production and managerial roles. But unlike many of Bruce's clients, fame and commercial success were not on Fahey's agenda. Instead, he wanted to make orchestral records that harkened back to Dixieland jazz.

Rather than continuing to explore the themes of the times, Fahey sought refuge in the uncoolest of pasts. Certainly no one would bother him there. However, the label seemed inflexible to opening a larger budget for such a project. "We started talking about the concept and I took the budget to Vanguard and they told me I was out of my mind, and that a Fahey LP was one microphone and a couple of rolls of tape," remembers Bruce. "I said that's what he does for Takoma, but that he's here to make a more commercial product. Fahey starts calling the owners of Vanguard at like four in the morning and bugging the shit out of them. So they dropped him from the label and fired me." However unceremonious a departure, his two LPs with the label helped bolster his popularity and established Fahey as a global artist with records distributed worldwide.

No longer selling records by the hundreds, he had become a commodity in the marketplace. He was interested in success and acclaim but only on his own terms; he would not sacrifice his musical vision for commercial considerations. "John felt he was ordained to be successful because of the innate musical quality of what he was doing," says Charters. And yet Denson, at Takoma, had a different perspective. "Ed made his living managing Country Joe," Charters continues. "He was very aware of the value of copyrights. He spent all his time talking to lawyers and paying bills." Takoma Records was operational and producing at an accelerating rate, yet Fahey seemed unsatisfied. Between his resentment of Country Joe & the Fish's success, his dismissal of Băsho, and his loss of aesthetic control over the label, Fahey decided that he no longer wanted to work with Denson and bought out his partner's shares in the label in late 1968. Their friendship had ended long before, and Denson and Fahey would never work together again.

Fahey moved the label to Los Angeles, slowly rebuilding it, and Jan took over managerial and accounting duties. With the streamlined efficiency of in-house management, the couple were able to make a decent living for themselves from the profits of the label, Fahey's performance proceeds, and record collecting.

VIEW EAST FROM THE TOP OF THE RIGGS ROAD B&O TRESTLE

"When a person is that ambitious they will invariably become disappointed in life. And they may hurt themselves and other people too with their ambition. And it is hard not to take the bait when there is a lot of money involved. But I was of the belief that everything usually comes to somebody that does very little or even nothing. All you have to do is not consider anything crucially important. Or urgent. It all comes down to he who waits."

—John Fahey, from *How Bluegrass Music Destroyed My Life*

Fahey once claimed to have been in a record store and seen a huge box of Bing Crosby's *White Christmas* LPs. The clerk told him they always sold out. This innocuous tale had strong reverberations for his career. In another step of anticool genius, Fahey concocted a concept for an album that resulted in his best selling and most famous work: *The New Possibility: John Fahey's Guitar Soli Christmas Album*. Released late in 1968, the album transcended genre and crossed over into the Christian market. People who had no concept of psychedelic or blues music bought the record for the acoustic renderings of "Joy to the

World" and "Silent Night," along with ancient European standards like "Greensleeves" thrown in for good measure. Presented on solo guitar, these Christmas tunes presaged the New Age movement. The album had vast appeal and would continue to sell seasonally for years after its release.

But Fahey continued to flaunt expectations: even a Christmas album was fair game as a place to vent. Fahey attacked many of the traditions of the holiday in his liner notes. Religion was a topic close to his heart, and he relished the chance to launch into a diatribe given the right platform. "Christmas and Easter are the two most important events of the Christian calendar, and should as such be celebrated with all due awe and respect, but not underneath a pagan Christmas tree, or in a department store, or by searching for the illusive commercial-divine EGG," wrote Fahey. While his criticism of the commercialism (written in the notes of a commercial product) of religion was certainly in line with similar ideas of the time, his ruthless attack on sentimentality extended even further. "I seriously doubt if the Son of Man ascended to Heaven on a rabbit," Fahey wrote. "I doubt if He sits on the right hand of Santa Claus. And children do not need to be told these things; it makes Christianity much less *possible* for them in later years. Superstition does not aid Christianity; it does not need it. Christianity is not a religion of superstition anyway, although you may think it is." His criticism stemmed from his reverence of religion and his respect for the mystery of the spiritual, yet it read as if he were delivering a sermon from a pulpit.

All theological debate aside, the album sold well into the six figures. Fahey seemed shocked by the success of *The New Possibility* and its far-reaching effects. He later recalled, "Well, the arrangements are pretty good, but on the other hand there are more mistakes on that album than on any of the other 17 albums I've recorded. And yet, here's the paradox . . . this album has not only sold more than any of my others, [but] I meet people all the time who are crazy about it. I mean really love it. What can I say? I'm confused." The Christmas album set a benchmark in sales for Fahey and ensured him live gigs and record deals for years to come.

There was also the business of a label to run. A year or so earlier, a demo tape had arrived at the Takoma offices from a guitar player no one there had heard of. Some dismissed it as sounding too much like Fahey. When the man himself heard the music, he was convinced of its commercial appeal. The tape, recorded by a young player named Leo Kottke, led to the biggest hit of either of their careers.

Born in Athens, Georgia, in 1945, Kottke had been a musician from a young age. Although he studied trombone as a kid, he found something far more substantial in the acoustic guitar. After a short stint in the navy, he hitchhiked around the United States, ending up in the Twin Cities in Minnesota. Kottke was still a teenager when he saw Robbie Băsho perform and became immediately enthralled by the artist's twelve-string technique. Kottke tried to corner him after the show and ask him questions, but Băsho had no interest in his newly minted fan. "Robbie'd just opened for someone, and that guy started playing back onstage while I babbled at Robbie," remembers Kottke. "Just a couple years ago I realized who that guy onstage was, I can still hear that big *bong* of a thumb on the E string as Robbie was running away from me. . . . It was Fahey. It was Fahey yet to be . . . which I'm thinking is all we'll ever know of him."

While Băsho ignored the eager fan, Fahey encouraged him. After discovering his tape, Fahey began a correspondence with the young midwesterner, and ended up taking him under his wing. Fahey tried to mold the young musician, encouraging Kottke not to sing but instead to concentrate on his instrumental work. Against conventional wisdom, the advice paid off when Kottke recorded an all-instrumental guitar album for Takoma. Though most labels likely encouraged vocals in order to sell records and get radio play, Kottke instead recorded the epic yet simply titled *6- and 12-String Guitar*. Released in 1969, Kottke's Takoma debut featured a high-energy, virtuosic display of guitar prowess and became the label's best-selling release, selling over half a million copies.

At the time, Fahey was still suffering from severe sleep deprivation. He had recently been overdoing it with his prescription sleep medications in an effort to combat his insomnia. The number of drugs required to get Fahey to sleep became massive. The results wreaked havoc on his already fragile mental state. He was often confused, and his moods raged while he attempted to combat his ailments. Even with Jan looking after him, he remained adrift in a sea of emotional chaos. Worse, his drinking was steadily growing. He was in such a stupor that he often forgot his concerts and his loud behavior; his blackouts grew in frequency and intensity. He had different doctors in various seedy parts of Los Angeles who refilled his prescriptions numerous times over. By telling them he was a musician set to go on tour he amassed stores of strong pharmaceuticals. When Kottke came to visit Fahey for the first time, shortly after his album's release, Fahey was completely dependent.

"John called me into the bathroom that first night at his place to show me what he needed to get to sleep, and to tell me, standing there in a sweat suit with a blindfold on his forehead and earplugs in his ears, not to wake him up," recalls Kottke. Fahey's isolation seemed bizarre to the young guitarist, who implicitly trusted his new mentor, even in the face of severe uncertainty. Fahey's letters to him were littered with swastikas and German, so he actually seemed more normal in person than in correspondence. "I can't figure how he survived as long as he did, but I do wonder," Kottke adds. "I saw him take two chloral hydrates, two or four 10 milligram Valiums, two 100 milligram Thorazines, a couple Placydyl. . . . He ate the pills in front of me and then exploded out of his bedroom an hour later, beet-red, yelling at me for waking him up with the television and waving a gun in my face. And it only happened once. And it just seemed normal. . . . John could do that."

The gun-toting incident didn't faze Kottke too much. Surviving that first night, he figured nothing worse could happen. He was right; afterward, Fahey became calm toward Kottke and enjoyed his company. The two got along well—they genuinely liked each other. "John had so much contempt for all his peers. He had no reason to even consider them on the same planet," says Charters. "Leo was an exception because he came under John's wing."

In public Kottke came off as a charming "everyman" kind of guy, lacking the immediately visible dysfunction of Fahey or Băsho. His onstage persona was far more relaxed, and he often told elaborate humorous stories between songs. As a humble midwesterner, his sincerity appealed to a broader demographic than his labelmates. Kottke was just happy to be in the game. His affability and charm translated to adoring audiences.

His lightning-fast playing made him an instant smash with tracks like the dizzying "Vaseline Machine Gun." In the process, Kottke cemented his status as a guitar icon with a singular album. The success also brought increased exposure to Takoma Records and, of course, Fahey. The pupil's success opened doors to new career opportunities for the master. And major record labels became aware of instrumental guitar music's potential to sell to a large commercial audience.

Though their business had grown exponentially since Fahey took it over outright, Jan still covered all aspects of it herself, from keeping the books to shipping boxes of records to distributors. In order to keep Kottke's album in stores, many other Takoma releases were left out of print for months or years, some never repressed at all. Whereas Băsho's sales floundered, Kottke became a sensation and Fahey felt vindicated in his A&R skills. Fahey was proud of himself for having the vision to see how successful his protégé would become, and Takoma Records had an influx of cash, enough to hire a ramshackle staff.

Fahey's peers were reaching new levels of success; both Country Joe & the Fish and Canned Heat made huge splashes at Woodstock and were off on promotional tours around the world, selling records and having hit songs on the radio. Country Joe had a number-one song with his antiwar anthem "I-Feel-Like-I'm-Fixin'-to-Die Rag," which catapulted sales of its Vanguard debut to over a million copies. Canned Heat had a top-thirty hit with "On the Road Again," sung by Al Wilson in a voice that recalls Skip James, and making him an unlikely pop singer. When Jan had taken over the books from Denson two years prior, Takoma was grossing $10,000 annually. After Kottke and *The New Possibility*, their yearly earnings had grown to $100,000. With a string of successes, Takoma was now on the radar of aspiring musicians and outside artists alike.

Labels in those days occasionally had artists stop by unannounced in an attempt to get noticed or to impromptu audition, especially in California. On one such occasion the Takoma office received a surprising visit from a group of unannounced guests. "These beautiful, young, scantily clad women showed up at the Takoma office with a one-inch demo tape that they wanted us to play," Fahey remembered. The young women claimed to live on a ranch in the desert and invited the staff to come see them there. They called themselves the Family. Acting on behalf of their spiritual leader, Charles

Manson, a frustrated musician who was a close associate of the Beach Boys until his aggressive ways alienated him from them, the girls sought Takoma as a potential new home for their guru's unreleased album. "Before they left those girls fucked everybody in the office, except me. And everybody in the office caught gonorrhea—except me. Later on we realized who they were," said Fahey. The rest of the world soon knew who they were, too, as names like Susan "Sadie Mae Glutz" Atkins and Lynette "Squeaky" Fromme eventually made international headlines. Although a relatively tame visit from the Manson Family—considering what they were capable of—the encounter certainly indicated that Takoma was growing in profile on the hippie scene.

As Fahey began to attract attention overseas, he made his debut European appearance in London. Britain had a huge traditional folk scene of its own, and the UK guitar elite turned out in droves to glimpse the mysterious John Fahey, the man behind Leo Kottke's Takoma album (by then, Kottke was a major headliner in the folk guitar world). Rather than dazzle the crowd with technical guitar playing, Fahey demonstrated his American Primitive technique to a less than spellbound audience. Among the artists in attendance were John Renbourn, John Martyn, Ralph McTell, Roy Harper, Mike Cooper, and Bert Jansch. Singer/guitarist Michael Chapman attended one of the London performances: "There was a famous club in London we all played called Les Cousins," he recalls. "That was the acoustic mafia's hideout. Fahey came and played and the back was wall-to-wall musicians. Everybody came to find out who this guy was, and he was dreadful. We kind of saw him as a one-off. No one else wanted to do what he was doing. We had English guys who were incredibly flashy, and that's what they had to do to satisfy an audience for an hour's performance. John saw things completely different. He would play as simply as he possibly could. He was doing that because that's what he believed in."

He may have been rejected by the guitar-playing community in London, but he immediately found fans within the music press. While in London on May 28, 1969, he recorded a session for John Peel's *Night Ride* show on BBC radio. Fahey revisited some of his earliest work, and the performance was a success. Peel was considered the preeminent tastemaker in British music culture, and his endorsement helped spread the music of Fahey to a wider audience abroad. Europe was filled with different social mores, which provided a whole new context in which Fahey could be misunderstood. This came to a head in the most traumatic failed collaboration of his professional career.

One morning in late 1969, Jan awoke him with an urgent telephone call. It was MGM Studios, on behalf of acclaimed Italian filmmaker Michelangelo Antonioni. Following his international breakthrough, *Blow Up*, Antonioni was riding high on his recent success. Antonioni was a fan of Fahey's records and wanted him to compose the soundtrack for his new movie, *Zabriskie Point*. The studio offered to fly Fahey first class to Italy the next morning to start work. Fahey had seen and enjoyed *Blow Up* and, at the urgings of his wife and management, he reluctantly agreed. Suspicious of things that seemed too good to be true and unaware of the expectations that he would need to live up to, he grew nervous.

Everyone in his camp seemed excited about the possibility except Fahey himself. With no prior preparation, he got on a plane to do a job for a man he had never met, on a film he knew nothing about. There are two distinct versions of what happened next. Fahey's version is extensively detailed in his memoir—and although almost entirely fictional, it gives a deeper insight into his psyche. His experience became one of the greatest stories in his mythology, a battle of wills that symbolized his contempt and misunderstanding of the culture in which he found himself. Just as in the blues, myths are often more important than the truth.

According to Fahey, when he arrived, he was greeted by handlers and eventually introduced to Antonioni himself, whom he described as "civilized and erudite and intelligent and polite and suave and sophisticated. Of course, now I know that those are the most dangerous kind of people that exist." Antonioni wanted him to create music for a group sex scene that had been shot out in the desert of California. He asked Fahey to echo the beauty of young love with the juxtaposition of death, to represent the emptiness of America and its celebrated youth culture. By no means a free spirit, Fahey had a terrible time viewing the twenty-minute sex scene. He found the proceedings sick and wanted no part of it.

Feeling as if he had been suckered into working on some high-end skin flick, he plotted his exit strategy. Since he was being paid by the day, and knowing that the overbudgeted studio would cater to any wild demand, Fahey booked several days of studio time with a group of local musicians. He instructed the group to improvise for hours; their only directive was to make sure the music never came together. They spent a few days making noise and enjoying the process on the company's dime. They ran out the clock unsupervised.

Rather than completely sabotage the project, he claimed to have recorded twenty minutes of solo guitar in a unique tuning that he felt actually summoned the love/death tension of the California desert. Having spent time in such climates while studying his beloved turtles, he had a connection to the bleak emptiness of the sparse, sprawling landscape. Confident that he had completed his task to the best of his abilities, he played the music for Antonioni, who declared it a rousing success.

With all parties placated, the project should have been resolved amicably. Things, however, fell apart when the two went out to celebrate at an upscale restaurant and began to talk politics. Antonioni started discussing how his film was a critique of American culture, which he thought was an abomination. In actuality, his and Fahey's views weren't that different. Fahey was hypercritical of the counterculture himself and wondered how anyone could live with it. His hangers-on nodded in agreement. Yet Fahey resented the director's insinuation that Americans were unsophisticated and endlessly materialistic. Perhaps in Antonioni's world this seemed the case, but Fahey resented the implied condescension. "I felt that my intelligence was insulted," wrote Fahey. "That, *qua* musician, I was being treated quite rudely and wrongly and unethically. I thought that this was an insult to my mind, my reality, my commitments, and everything that I was, and everything that I stood for."

Despite his similar objections to excess and hedonism, Fahey decided he wanted nothing to do with what he perceived as an anti-American propaganda film. Being the patriot that he was, he felt it his duty to stand up and defend his homeland. The disagreement escalated, and the two began shouting in the restaurant. Then Fahey punched the famed director in the face. The two never spoke again. Fahey's music was cut from the film—though he was still paid for his work—and was replaced with Jerry Garcia and Pink Floyd songs. The film was considered a disappointment upon release, and Fahey felt vindicated by its commercial failure.

This entire account, as recalled by Fahey in his memoir, is actually a piece of revisionist history, a product of his wild imagination. "If he had done anything like that he would have been arrested on the spot," says Jan. "I think people believe what they want to believe." While Fahey did indeed travel to Rome on the director's behest, no sort of confrontation occurred. He became so blocked by the whole experience that he couldn't produce anything. He drank to the point where he was stumbling around and practically incoherent, according to Jan, who had accompanied him. The reality of the situation was that Fahey faced creative impotency and failed to compose any music. Always one to attempt to recontextualize the events of his life, Fahey rewrote his failure as that of rebellion and toughness, a nod to his teenage greaser persona. At the time, those in his camp excited about the prospect of the collaboration found their hopes dashed. And with them, a great opportunity for his career to progress beyond his 1960s cult status was lost.

More troublesome was his psychological state after returning home. Jan recalls that his delicate condition crossed the line into full-fledged breakdown. "By the time he got home he had a psychotic break," says Jan. "He was just completely out of it. He was taking more and more of his drugs, he was drinking heavily, he didn't know where he was, he didn't know who I was." He started suffering from increasingly elaborate delusions. "He believed he was possessed by demons," recalls Jan. "That this is what was causing all these problems. He thought he was *actually* possessed by demons. He saw an orange snake. There were others. He saw them when he was awake."

His daily care had become a full-time responsibility, and Jan and her family sought help at a mental clinic in Santa Monica. He stayed there for about a month. When he returned, things at home were difficult; the marriage was severely troubled. "Fahey and I had dinner at her parents' house," remembers manager Denny Bruce. "They were extremely nice—nice home, she's great and here's this guy with blue jeans and a denim shirt sitting at the table not really talking. Maybe Jan was crazy? I was polite to the parents and everything. She must know something I don't because she was putting up with it."

Meanwhile, Takoma hired a full-time employee, Jon Monday, who first came aboard to fill orders (he would become the label's longest-standing employee). As a Fahey fan, he was aware of the artist beforehand. "I didn't know what to expect when I first met him. I greatly admired his records, so I was a bit awestruck. John was just plain folk. He had no sense of self-importance," recalls Monday. "Jeans, T-shirt, and tennis shoes was his typical dress code—at home, in the office, in the studio, or onstage." Monday, who had garnered some major-label promotions work, was eventually hired to take on the task of publicity for Takoma and for Fahey. "I developed a mailing list, went to local [radio] stations, and traveled on the road with John to promote his concerts and the records. I'd contact the local radio stations, get them to play John's records, and occasionally I'd get him an on-air interview. I was the director of promotion." They also added Kerry Fahey, a young man of no relation—though John often told people that Kerry was his cousin and treated him accordingly—to help with filling orders.

Never one to suffer fools lightly, Fahey could be combative with the media, especially those unfamiliar with his work. Monday recalls one incident: "I had arranged to get him on a music TV show in L.A. called *Headshop*, that was hosted by Elliot Mintz. I think Joan Baez was also on that same episode. Anyway, John was supposed to 'lip-sync' his guitar playing—they would play the record, and John would look like he was playing live. John was shown where to sit and get ready to play. The camera was on Elliot, who did the introduction: 'And here's John Fahey to sing a song off his latest album.' The camera is switched to John. John shouted, 'I don't sing songs. This guy doesn't even know who I am!' They had to stop the taping, reset the positions and cameras. John started pretending to play the song, but then started swinging his right arm wildly, like Pete Townshend. I'm sure it pissed everyone off, but John didn't care. I, of course, was worried about the effect on his career from these outbursts."

Later that year *Rolling Stone* magazine decided to profile Fahey for a feature story. The ever-candid subject was only too happy to open up regarding his personal instability. In the December 24, 1970, issue, writer Tim Ferris found his subject in a suitable state of disarray. "Fahey hasn't made a record in two years, since he did *Yellow Princess* on Vanguard and *Voice of the Turtle* [and *The New Possibility*] on Takoma," wrote Farris. "During the first of those two years he was known as a man who would take a drink. During the second, he could be found three times a week in the office of a psychiatric ward in Santa Monica." Fahey left the impression of a man in trouble and on the verge of collapse. "I was really crazy, like, back in February. I was really nuts," he told Farris. "There's a whole sequence that I can't remember. One day I woke up thinking I was going to go crazy. I thought, 'Well, I'll sit this out for a couple of days.' Then that night I thought 'hmmmm, I'd better go to sleep or I'll go crazy. . . .' But I couldn't. I was going to kill myself. Then Jan stole my gun. It really made me mad. I felt kind of suicidal. I looked for the gun and the gun was gone. Somehow I got over to St John's Hospital in Santa Monica."

While most artists would attempt to shield their violent, suicidal dysfunctions, Fahey chose to highlight them to the reporter. In the chaos of the times, though, this went largely unnoticed. The dark side of excess touched those close to Fahey as well. Lost in the throes of success, Canned Heat guitarist and close friend Al Wilson died of a drug overdose. His death at a young age was a harbinger of counterculture decay that would soon become a cliché. They had long talked of Wilson doing a solo album for Takoma, but it never would be. "I will remember Wilson . . ." he wrote. "Of course because he was my roommate for about half a year. How could I forget his odor? And how could I forget the wonderful music he played and sang? And how could I forget all the things he taught me about music? That would be impossible."

Fahey returned to audiences in 1971 with the sprawling *America*, a record that reinforced his stature. Opening with a harmonic minimalism, Fahey barred the twelfth fret, creating a chiming by holding his finger lightly over the strings while his right hand repeated a pattern. In New York, minimalist composers like Terry Riley and Steve Reich were gaining favor by employing similar repetitive techniques in their compositions. Fahey, using the acoustic guitar, created an album that stands alongside any long-form composition of the times in terms of scope and approach. Originally intended to be released as a double LP, Fahey cut *America* down by half at the last moment when he decided that a double LP was a harder sell than a single. With the album already in the test-pressing phase, Fahey decided to randomly pull one of the two LPs outright.

While the majority of his Takoma releases had been hodgepodge assemblies of home recordings, this album was recorded at Larrabee Sound Studios in Los Angeles and features a clarity and tone that captures his performances immaculately. His classical influences again arise in the structure and makeup of his pieces. While it isn't new territory, the album represents a perfection of his stylistic combinations. He references his older pieces, revisiting their themes on "Mark 1:15," which for years would be one of his favorite songs to play live. "Out of all the songs I ever wrote, I consider only two of them 'epic' or 'classic' or in the 'great' category and they are both on this record," Fahey said of *America*. "Most of the melodic ideas existed a long time ago, i.e. the primary 'lyric' melody in 'Mark 1:15' is the same as 'When the Springtime Comes Again' . . ." The album ends with a take on Sam

McGee's "Knoxville Blues," which resolves the record on a traditional note. With a theme of ecological conservation in the album's artwork, no liner notes accompanied the music. Instead a series of surreal, symbolic drawings by friend Pat Finnerty narrate the story of the poisoning of an ancient turtle that lived in the Adelphi Mill Pond back in Takoma Park. Both front and back covers feature a turtle fleeing the destruction of man. Fahey wrote elsewhere of the situation:

> There is a pulp-mill somewhere in Maryland. And this mill pours its refuse into what is now, but was not always, a land-locked lake. And in that lake lived an enormous turtle, (only one) very old, very large, his shell painted by moss and pulp. You can (or at least I can) hear his voice, or rather cry, sometimes late at night when everything else is still. He was there long before the mill came. The water is bad now, but there are still a few carp and cat-fish on the bottom for him to snap up and chomp on. For some reason no one else has ever seen him, and as an amateur herpetologist I should like to say that he resembles no species that I have ever seen or heard of elsewhere. There he spends his days confined to the polluted water. There is no outlet. He cannot make it to the sea. Nothing ever gets out of that lake. He basks and sounds, half conscious, half asleep, half alive, the first and last of his kind. The workers in the mill do not bother him; they mistake him for an old log. He waits for death in the dirty water but doesn't even think about the waiting. He is an old turtle, and having seen the horizon on all sides, there is not much more for him to think about. I used to go and watch him. He saw me too, I think. Sometimes I imagined we understood something of each other. But I could never tell what it was.

On the home front, following Fahey's release from the hospital, he and Jan attempted in vain to save their marriage. In the spring of 1971 they tried couples counseling. After a few sessions Fahey started going by himself. He was getting slightly better and even started to dress in suits for the first time. One night he decided to take Jan for a night on the town sporting his new look. He seized the opportunity to have some fun. "John started feeling better about himself, instead of wearing jeans and a blue work shirt, which he wore the entire time I knew him, he got himself a suit and tie, button-down shirts, and all this stuff," Jan remembers. "We went to the Troubadour and he took a cane and wore dark glasses and was bumping into people as if he was blind. That was John."

With Kottke a runaway success, manager Denny Bruce had more leverage in which to create new business opportunities. Several plans were in the works for Fahey and Takoma. They hatched an idea to use Bruce's connections to get Kottke a home at a major record label, with Fahey and Bruce attached as producers under the banner Takoma Productions. Bruce shopped the deal to Capitol Records and sold the three of them as a package. In 1971, they began work on Kottke's Capitol debut, *Mudlark*, with Canned Heat's Larry Taylor on bass and a session drummer. Every time Kottke began to play, Fahey stopped him and asked him to retune or start over. Feeling the pressure, Kottke grew stressed at having to perform in front of a hypercritical Fahey. Bruce stepped in to try to rectify the situation.

"After half an hour of not letting him play a verse all the way through, Leo is at the breaking point," remembers Bruce. "He asks to see me in the hallway and says he can't record with John there. It was intimidating that he kept stopping him and criticizing his guitar sound, he couldn't concentrate. He wanted the chance to make the record with the session musicians there. I took John aside and told him he was intimidating Leo and to just let me produce it myself, and that he would get the same money and not have to show up. He got a beaming smile on his face and said it was the best news he heard all year." Fahey fussed around for about an hour and took off. "It shocked me that John would want to produce anything, so it was no surprise when he split, but I was envious," recalls Kottke. "I remember his expression as he walked out: frozen." Without Fahey, the album became a moderate major-label success. Kottke spent the next few decades on a stable career path, which continued to subsidize Fahey and Bruce through their publishing arrangements.

Fahey's improvements from therapy with Jan were short-lived and mostly cosmetic. Rather than see himself as a person who had problems that needed to be solved, he became enthralled by his own fascinating tapestry of dysfunction. He found his neuroses and their sources to be of endless interest. Jan didn't want to indulge him, and saw that there seemed little chance for a life for herself within the marriage. Fahey needed constant care and attention, and she could no longer handle the burden. They soon separated and Jan moved out. "Every day was something else, and he was really sick, the poor guy," says Jan. "It was miserable. The mood swings and all the booze and the pills and not sleeping. I didn't know how to help him. I didn't hate him. It got to the point where neither of us knew what to do. That was the worst. That was the lowest part of the whole thing. Even after I moved out, I used to take food over there three times a day. I couldn't abandon him, but I couldn't live with him either."

Post-separation life was difficult for Fahey. He lived with "cousin" Kerry Fahey for a time. Jan and Kerry tried their best to get John off of drugs, once even flushing the contents of all his pill bottles down the toilet. An irate Fahey went ballistic and the police had to be called to calm him down. When Jan told them about the situation they suggested she calm him down with liquor—hardly a productive solution for an alcoholic. His proposed solution to their problems was for the two of them to run away to the woods and retreat from the pressures of society. He thought that if they lived alone and isolated, his hysteria would be calmed and he'd be better able to function. For her own sake, she decided to divorce him.

Jan's visits became less frequent. She had dreams of her own beyond that of taking care of her husband, isolated from the rest of the world. "My life was going by and I was taking care of this man who I can't help that was getting worse and I felt like I needed to get out to save my own sanity, but I felt bad about abandoning him," she remembers.

When they officially divorced in 1973, Fahey grew angry. Remembering his fury over his split with Pat Sullivan, Jan decided it would be best to cut off contact with him completely. They never spoke again, although he later recalled her fondly. Fahey's extremes were too much to sustain his marriage, and his divorce would be costly, both for lawyers and in his settlement to Jan. Over the next few years, her share of Takoma was bought out, and Fahey pressed forward.

OLD FASHIONED LOVE

"All I have ever done with music was to depict various emotions in an organized and coherent musical language, especially hate, fear, repulsion, grief, depression or feeling nothingness."

—John Fahey, in his liner notes to *The Legend of Blind Joe Death*, 1996 reissue of *Blind Joe Death*

Inspired by the movie *The Traveling Executioner*, a dark comedy set in the South, Fahey and Bruce decided to focus on the traditional southern jazz experience for Fahey's next record, using original musicians from the 1920s as session players to add authenticity. The eventual lineup included Nappy Lamare on banjo and Jack Feierman on trumpet along with some contemporary studio musicians such as Chris Darrow (who played with James Taylor and Leonard Cohen) and Joel Druckman (Bonzo Dog Band) to even things out. Through Bruce's connections, Fahey signed to Reprise Records, an imprint of Warner Brothers started by Frank Sinatra. "Warner's was still thinking that if enough people told them something was cool, let's say Rambin' Jack Elliot or Ed Sanders from the Fugs," they'd sign them, says Bruce.

"These guys got deals too. John Fahey, sure, very well known, very influential. How much do these guys really sell?"

The label was able to foot the hefty bill for the recordings, unlike Vanguard, which had scoffed when approached with the same idea. However, the process was not without its share of difficulties. "You had to get Fahey when he was in a good mood and wanted to have fun," remembers Bruce. "Recording with the engineer and the other musicians for the Warner Brothers albums, he would be late sometimes. He'd have this ritual where he'd go in the bathroom for half an hour and wash his fingerpicks in soap and have to line them up one by one on paper towels on top of the sink. I'd ask him what we're waiting for and he'd say that the picks had to dry so they feel right. Then he came out and would smoke a cigarette and drink an entire liter of Pepsi and not say anything, just sitting there. The engineer and I had been waiting there for three hours already; all you could hope for is that he would get them in one take."

Rather than expanding on his more experimental work, Fahey opted for an album of mostly straight versions of Dixieland jazz standards. For an artist who seemed so conceptually modern, the resulting *Of Rivers and Religion* album felt antiquated and out of step, especially for an artist once vehemently opposed to revivalism. "When John began working with Dixieland musicians I was really disappointed," says Sam Charters. "To me those records were just the pits." Credited to John Fahey and His Orchestra, the album cover pictured a black-and-white photo of an old-time riverboat that looked as if it had been torn from the pages of an old book. Fahey actually took the picture himself at Disney World. It was a plastic simulation of antiquated themes, much like the album itself. The elaborate Dixieland band sounds enough like the real thing, but it is still only a copy. There is no integration of stylistic forms; rather it is played straight, with a slightly slow drawl.

Still, several solo performances by Fahey resound with despair and raw beauty, such as "Funeral Song for Mississippi John Hurt," a reworked and improved version of the cut found on *Requia*. Without his "orchestra," he still shines, sounding even crisper with studio-quality recording; but with them, he seems drowned out. These profound solo moments were sparse amid the horn blasts of Tin Pan Alley bombast. He accomplished his goal of making Dixieland ensemble music and remained true to his vision, but the record never found an audience beyond his die-hard fans.

In the liner notes, *Village Voice* critic Nat Hentoff wrote, "I was not prepared for what I heard in this album. I've been absorbed in all kinds of music for a long time, and only rarely have the first few notes of a musician I'm listening to for the first time announced a wholly singular presence—an event." But there were very few who found the record as thrilling. Although Fahey's excitement about the material was sincere, the results came off as campy to many, and accordingly, it suffered from minimal sales. At a concert in San Francisco soon after the album's release, Reprise's head of A&R, Gary George, complained to Bruce that Fahey was boring.

Working within the major-label recording industry, Fahey still refused to make compromises, artistically or politically. One of his favorite venues was an auditorium at UC Santa Barbara, which he always sold out. The promoter asked Bruce, as Fahey's manager, if Asylum Records recording artist David Blue could do a short opening set. Blue shared the same manager as Neil Young, and the promoter was looking to earn some points to get Young shows in the future. Fahey had known Blue from New York and agreed. "We're backstage and John is going through his ritual, washing his guitar picks, and Joni Mitchell walks in with her two managers via a limo," remembers Bruce. "She wanted to go out and play a few extra songs with David

Blue. Nobody had cleared this with me. Fahey is looking at his watch and is now mentally ready to go on and he walked over to Joni Mitchell and said, 'You're not going out there tonight. Sorry.' Her managers started in on him—David Geffen was one of them; Elliot Roberts, who was Neil Young's manager, was the other—saying, 'Do you know who we are?' etc. Elliot Roberts said something that really pissed him off and Fahey said, 'If you don't get your ass and hers out of here in two minutes I'm going to beat the fucking shit out of you.' They hightailed it out of there. Fahey says, 'Who does she think she is? She tried to do this to me before at Swarthmore College. They purposely came late so she could play after me. She has how many albums out? Two or three? Well I have twenty, so fuck her.' That's the maddest I've ever seen him."

Fahey remained at odds with a universe that didn't consider him a priority. Although the performances and recordings were rich and dynamic, *Of Rivers and Religion* seemed like a crucial misstep, a floundered opportunity to capitalize on the major-label exposure and distribution of Reprise. Fahey still steadfastly had no interest in considering commercial appeal; he followed his muse no matter how it affected his career. As long as he could make a living creating records, that was enough for him.

It remains something of a miracle that the label agreed to foot the bill for a follow-up, the equally disappointing *After the Ball*, in 1973. The sequel also featured jazz accompanists. Not surprisingly, it tanked just as badly, ending his major-label run. "We were left alone to do what we wanted, and that's what he wanted," says Bruce. "Well, how many John Fahey albums had already been made by then? This was the next one. I knew I was in trouble when they only pressed two thousand copies."

Still, Fahey had cemented his reputation as an iconic instrumentalist, and his achievements continued to garner him attention from aspiring musicians. Among those who sought his counsel was a pianist named George Winston. Thrilled at the idea of an artist releasing instrumental music on his own terms, Winston brought a copy of his demos of solo piano recordings to one of Fahey's concerts. "The show was at the Paul Masson winery, and John played first and Dave Van Ronk played second," remembers Winston. "He didn't say anything the whole time, would just go into the next piece. At one point an airplane went by and he sort of stared at it like it was interfering with the show. Everybody just laughed."

Afterward, Fahey asked to hear some of Winston's demos and played them right there. Much to Winston's surprise, Fahey instantly offered him a deal with Takoma. "John was doing everything I wanted to be doing. Playing solo instrumental concerts," says Winston. "He was recording other solo acoustic guitarists and he was making his own instrumental records. Those were all things I saw in myself and I couldn't believe anyone else was doing it. Not only had he recorded Băsho, Kottke, and Peter Lang, but he thought piano fit into that. There was no one else in the world that would have recorded me at that time. Solo piano at the beginning of the glam rock era? I couldn't believe it. John came down when I recorded it in '72 and I did the final sessions alone. He was there at the studio but he kind of just read comic books while me and the engineer talked. It was real casual." The resulting *Ballads and Blues* received minimal sales or attention, but it started Winston on the path to becoming a multiplatinum-selling artist in the soon-to-come New Age market.

Fahey's effect as an artist and label owner began drawing other musicians into his orbit. He continued to eschew praise whenever it came his way. Winston once made the mistake of referring to him as a great composer and Fahey refused to speak to him, accusing him of being a groupie. "Now everyone calls him a composer," adds Winston.

"He just wasn't ready to see himself that way [then], but I saw it right away. He was a great composer, not a great guitarist. Then after a few months, I guess he forgot, and we went back to being normal people, but of course he was right."

In spite of his disdain for behavior he saw as sycophantic, even Fahey could be blown away. He was extremely particular about what he liked, but when he found music that moved him he became swept up in the excitement. At a live performance of Brazilian guitarist Bola Sete, Fahey experienced a life-altering musical moment. Sete was best known for playing with jazz great Dizzy Gillespie, but his solo compositions were textured, rich with flourish and emotion. Using space and subtle shifts of rhythm, his songs had a more compositional feel than those of players on the folk scene, perhaps because his Brazilian roots lent him techniques and phrasings that were untouched by American players of the time. Meeting Sete after the show, Fahey asked him about the secret to his playing. Sete recommended meditation.

Fahey wrote about the experience at length in a characteristically confessional editorial for *Guitar Player* in the early 1970s. Fahey described first seeing Sete play in San Francisco circa 1972 while intoxicated. He went on to reveal that he had been high on drugs, daily for many years, and, in his own words, "walking and talking amongst the shadows." The purity of Sete's playing left him changed, much like his initial experience with the blues. "Few living people have had such an enormous influence on my life, my music, my soul, my religion—you name it—as has Bola Sete," Fahey wrote.

Awed by his prowess, Fahey asked Sete to record for Takoma. Tucked away in Sete's archive was a solo guitar album he had recorded that had been rejected by other labels. A few years later, Takoma issued Sete's *Ocean*, and for the rest of his life Fahey called it his favorite solo guitar record.

Sete's playing was separate from the blues influence that trapped so many others. With this new influence, Fahey envisioned different directions and stylistic innovations. He longed for the same spiritual center that Sete evoked in his music. Upon discovering that the secret to Sete's intensity was meditation, he sought to cleanse himself of toxins. He believed that they distracted him, preventing him from communicating honestly through his music. Quitting his prescription pill habit, he turned to transcendental meditation.

To facilitate his newfound sobriety, he began attending Krishna temples around L.A. He found the rituals spellbinding. The services reminded him of one of his favorite silent films, *The Thief of Bagdad*. "They had a service every day with singing and horns and amplified harmonium," Fahey recalled. "I'd go over there just for the beauty of it. I didn't believe in Krishna or anything." He seemed comfortable being a religious tourist, taking solace in the ritual.

His new interest found its way onto his records as he continued to move away from shorter, song-based pieces to extended sidelong compositions. Fahey showcased this approach on his next Takoma album, *Fare Forward Voyagers*. Released in 1973, during the hangover of the 1960s rock 'n' roll crash, the album feels like a spiritual retreat. It marks a departure from his earlier material, featuring long-form ragas of alternating rhythms and tempos. The album finds him at the height of his prowess, delivering deeply hypnotic performances. The nuances of his fingerpicking combined with his stylistic integrations of American and Indian music made for a fully developed album. Dedicating the album to his guru, the record contained a pamphlet for the "Yogaville West" retreat with an endorsement by Fahey printed on it. "I would like to introduce you to this healthy, spiritually based concept of living. The 46 people living here follow the ideals of Integral Yoga as taught by Swami Satchidananda. To the extent that I have practiced these techniques, they really seem to work." These were his only words for the album; no stories or fiction found their way in. Takoma Park, for once, seemed out of view.

He never returned to this style of long-form playing, which makes *Fare Forward Voyagers* unique in his catalog. The compositions were difficult for him to reproduce live, although he did perform the bulk of the material in a stellar performance at Carnegie Hall on September 21, 1973, as part of an evening of guitar music along with sets by classical guitarist Laurindo Almeida and jazz player Gabor Szabo. Upon being introduced to the audience, Fahey barely acknowledged the crowd and launched into his set. After one continuous half-hour piece he picked his head up and was met with thunderous applause. Performing solo guitar at one of the world's premier cultural institutions, he had unquestionably succeeded in his initial musical goal, bringing his style of American Primitive guitar playing to the heights of the cultural elite.

With Jan out of the picture, Fahey restructured Takoma. He wanted nothing to do with the actual business aside from choosing records, so he put Jon Monday's friend Charlie Mitchell in charge. The label threw together a compilation album featuring tracks from three of its star guitarists—Fahey, Kottke, and new arrival to Takoma Peter Lang. It became another top seller.

With business steady, Fahey hired new employees to run the day-to-day. "John could have run it, but he didn't want to," remembers Monday. "John knew I was friends with Charlie, whose office was in the same building as Takoma. John asked me if Charlie could be trusted; I said yes—not that my vote counted for much. Charlie was hired as president and given a deal for a third of the company. We got a real entertainment lawyer and accountant for the first time. We had steady sales growth from 1970 to about 1976 or even

1977. We repromoted the Fahey Christmas album, Kottke's *6- and 12-String Guitar* (the label's two best sellers), and released a Mike Aldridge LP and the Kottke-Fahey-Lang album."

Fahey found recognition in other far-flung reaches of the creative arts as well. In 1971, Stanley Kubrick notably gave Fahey's 1965 album *The Transfiguration of Blind Joe Death* prominent placement in the record store scene of his classic film *A Clockwork Orange.* Fahey received letters of admiration from Kubrick and rock stars like Pete Townshend. Fahey reportedly replied to the Who star with a letter specifically detailing why the *Tommy* album was not, in fact, an opera.

Meanwhile, Fahey was dating a woman named Marilyn, with whom he had a volatile relationship. Fahey had been playing an extremely rare Ray Whitley Recording King guitar, a beautiful vintage instrument coveted by acoustic players. Once, backstage at a concert, the two began a heated argument. Marilyn stepped on the guitar. Fahey became so furious that he screamed that she should finish the job, then promptly took the guitar and smashed it to pieces.

Yet despite, or perhaps because of, Fahey's inability to control his emotions, he intensified his focus on healthy living. Yoga became his central philosophy. When keeping the routine of constant practice, he achieved his goal of staying sober. Some have described the environment of Yogaville as "cultlike," with its devout followers of the spiritual guru. Yet yoga provided a great opportunity to meet girls as well. In 1974, Yogaville hired a young woman named Deborah Goldman to organize a concert at the Wiltern Theatre for the swami's sixtieth birthday. Scheduled to appear were Carlos Santana, Alice Coltrane, and Fahey. Goldman started receiving bouquets of red roses until they filled an entire room at Yogaville. Fahey sent them—after meeting her just once. Eleven years younger than the then thirty-five-year-old Fahey, Goldman, who had turned down graduate school for a job at the institute, went along with it—apprehensively. Although overwhelmed by his aggressive pursuit, the two connected and started dating. "He was funny, he was smart, interesting, intellectual, obviously talented if you like music, which I do," says Goldman.

What truly bonded them was their lifestyle, dedicated to the teachings of the swami. "At the time we had this spiritual interest in yoga; more than just the physical exercises it was a philosophy, a way of living." The temple encouraged their relationship, as both were active members. Fahey seemed to represent the opposite of a dull, standard life for Goldman. Temporarily, things seemed as if they could work between the couple. With the structure of yoga to keep him sober and the thrill of a new romance, he remained stable and content. He soon proposed to Goldman and she accepted, if somewhat reluctantly. The Swami Satchidananda married them at a friend's house in Santa Barbara on January 1, 1975.

The quick courtship and subsequent romance wouldn't yield a long-lasting union. Fahey's relationship ideas were far from Goldman's. She had career ambitions in the age of women's liberation and quickly became bored killing time in between Fahey's jobs. "I married John, and for me to just hang out at the house was not consistent with my character so I took the real estate exam. I was going to work with this really successful friend who I knew in the field, but John didn't even like the idea of me working. That was also a source of tension," Goldman says. Considering the other person in a relationship seemed more than Fahey was capable of; he needed to be the focal point. "Having known other musicians, I think their emotions are close to the surface and they very much have an interior life that is self-centered to the extent that it's all they are focused on," continues Goldman. "I think that makes it difficult [for them] to have relationships."

As the 1970s progressed, so did the demands of touring. Fahey settled into the role of cult figurehead and possessed an untouchable prestige that came with a decade-plus run of successful musical innovations. Yet he still rejected careerism. "He would always compare himself to Leo [Kottke], who was the trouper who went out there and killed every night," says Denny Bruce. "Fahey just called him 'superstar' and said he wasn't interested in being a superstar. He didn't want to do the industry thing and be interviewed and have pictures taken of him. He didn't want to play the game—the politics to work with the right promoters and venues and so on and so forth. He was just as happy to play for promoter Sandy Getz in a little club. Sandy had been at the Ash Grove, where John used to play a lot before [Santa Monica folk club] McCabe's opened, and Sandy started booking some jazz guys and would also book John. It wasn't Carnegie Hall, but she'd pay him a few hundred dollars and he was happy with that."

Fahey's fan base seemed to be the same loyal listeners who saw him each time he came through town. Uncomfortable with the process of performing live, he was able to get through shows and impress audiences and critics—even if he barely acknowledged their presence. The *New York Times* championed Fahey for a mid-1970s concert, head pop critic John Rockwell writing, "John Fahey, who stopped by the Bottom Line for two shows Sunday night, remains as impressive and distinctive a master of the acoustic guitar as he ever was."

His performances throughout the 1970s occasionally eclipsed his albums and left audiences spellbound. One never knew which Fahey would arrive; the highs and lows of his temperament made for unreliable but sporadically sublime concerts. Still, he could rely on the reputation he spent much of the former decade establishing and still channel the cool, detached 1950s rebel bit he cultivated in high school. In a review of a concert at Hunter College in New York in 1975, the

Village Voice's Paul Nelson sums up his intimidating persona: "His guitar-playing is a deliberate mixture of psychology, order, mythology, poetry, and genre—all very exact, with the meaning entirely between the lines. Part of our fine national school of minimal acting, glints of feeling shining through the stoic, awesome professionalism that is characteristic of the American hero, John Fahey seems to me to be the Clint Eastwood/Steve McQueen of the guitar. I'd hate to meet him in a dark alley. He didn't even say goodbye."

By the mid-1970s, Fahey fell into a professional routine, finding ample touring work both in the States and abroad. His music had particular appeal to European audiences, as its instrumentalism presented no language barrier to overcome, speaking even to those who had no knowledge of the personal exorcisms he presented in his liner notes. One of his European tours had him paired up with Michael Chapman for several weeks, playing throughout Germany. "The folk and acoustic scene in Germany was huge at that time. There was a club in every town. Quite big audiences, three hundred or four hundred people a night in seated theaters. John at this time was a kind of legendary figure. He could make that fucking thing dance. It was just a joy when he got it right," recalls Chapman. Chapman remembers Fahey more as the absent-minded professor, a genius in his own world, however clumsily he stumbled through life. These shows produced his next generation of fans. While not hippies, many of these listeners were seeking relaxing music, an escape from the excess of 1970s stadium rock music.

His career may have been self-sustaining, but his marriage was dissolving. After a few months on the road, Goldman found, Fahey became a different man when separated from the peaceful environment of the Yoga Institute. His fears and temperament were impossible to contain, and his venomous contempt for touring life poisoned the new marriage. His anxiety and stress cast a dark shadow over their travels together. "I like to travel and I like music. The clubs were fun, but I think that was the downfall of the marriage because John did not enjoy performing. He had stage fright, which made him anxious and stressed out and it kind of deteriorated the relationship when we were on the road," says Goldman. "He was hard for me to be around. A more mature person might have had the tools to help, but I wasn't used to being around someone like that. I didn't particularly want to be around someone like that. I don't think I had the motivation to try to figure it out or make it work."

The couple temporarily lived in New York City between tours. When John left for a few days of shows, Deborah headed back west. Fahey seemed furious, according to her friends, and they never spoke again. According to Fahey's tour manager at the time, Stephen Calt, Deborah and Calt had struck up a romance while commiserating about the difficulties of dealing with the troubled guitarist. In the face of Fahey doing nothing to save the marriage, she took off with Calt. Upon hearing about the alleged tryst, Fahey drove around searching for Goldman, carrying a gun. He also called Calt's girlfriend, looking for the two. After a few months of delayed correspondence, all three went their separate ways without further incident.

His personal life changed profoundly again that year when he met a young woman at a Joseph Byrd concert named Melody Brennan. As a self-described Jungian, she clashed with the strict Freudian methodology Fahey had adopted during his split with Jan, but they found plenty else in common. A child of the San Fernando Valley, she grew up in California, eventually studying in the UCLA film program. (Jim Morrison was among her classmates there.) She spent the next twelve years working on various film-related educational projects. Melody had an artistic streak, which included painting and music.

It was Fahey's charm and sense of humor that again won him the girl. "John was always a very funny person with a great sense of humor. He was very intelligent and attractive in a lot of ways because of those things," she recalls. For fun they rode their bikes around to local Hare Krishna temples and visited the neighborhood cats. Fahey brought a mouse on a string and played games with cats they encountered. Melody soon began accompanying him on tour, selling his records at the concerts. In between they stopped at zoos and aquariums, both of which Fahey loved. They liked to visit museums as well, but Fahey didn't like to walk, so Melody would stroll around while he waited on a bench. They would also shop on the road, Fahey for records and Melody for antiques. It was a lifestyle that worked for both of them. "John was a dynamic person, just like his music," she adds. "He would go from quiet and gentle to raging loud and back and down and around. That was his music and that was his personality, too. He was interesting. You were never bored around John."

With American culture in a postrevolutionary lull, the often beautiful and contemplative music of John Fahey remained relevant and engaging to audiences. Because it had no roots in the political agendas of any time, his already extensive discography continued to be discovered by new listeners, particularly young guitar players. Fahey's slow, even pace and open tunings made the guitar more approachable to beginners; it was a style easy to emulate.

Fahey was fundamentally uncomfortable with his status as a technician. While the language of guitar is often spoken in notes, phrasings, and chords, Fahey was far more interested in the emotions behind such choices than the process itself. "When I play the guitar, even when I am practicing, I am besieged with images, memories, déjà vu experiences and emotions; and for every chord I play, for every tune I write, there is within me a distinct and unique image, emotion, or feeling," he wrote.

No one embodied the professional, technical guitar player better than Stefan Grossman, a blues fanatic and guitar player who came up around the same time as Fahey and became active during the folk resurgence of the early 1960s. Grossman, who never had much success in the commercial world, became a guitar teacher after several years of study with the gospel/blues master guitarist Reverend Gary Davis. Grossman studied various guitar techniques and began publishing a series of instructional books. The kind of player who rarely missed a note, he concentrated on the minute details of transposition and notation. Grossman seemed ideally suited for the task of publishing guitar notation guides.

In Fahey's mind, there existed little content in Grossman's work beyond the appreciation of traditional technique. He let his opinions of Grossman be known openly, naming a track on his 1976 LP *Old Fashioned Love*, "The Assassination of Stephan Grossman," most likely intentionally misspelling the name. Fahey, after much pestering, was convinced to participate in transcribing his own compositions in a *Best of John Fahey* guitar tablature book. Takoma released an LP of the same name in conjunction with the book, a compilation of early Fahey favorites. He had largely abandoned his lengthy prose in his albums' liner notes, but he seized upon the opportunity in his book of guitar tablature to mount a massive tirade against the conformity and rigidity of technical guitar playing. The result is a bizarre ramble that mixes guitar-playing tips with gender politics and confessional therapy. "Mastering a guitar is really very similar to conquering a woman, and when you fail to master it, like when you fail to master a woman, you have the same feelings of humiliation and violence," wrote Fahey. "When you are alone with your guitar, you must win if you are to be a man."

These life lessons on machismo were not exactly what most young students were looking for in an instructional book. More sage advice was his advocacy of playing for many hours at a time to trick the mind to try new things out of sheer boredom, to force the creative to take over. Only in this mental trance, he wrote, can the link to the unconscious be achieved. This language can't be explained with notes or transcriptions, but he sought to relay his example to those who wanted to know something about existential guitar. "What I am advocating is the supremacy of playing by ear and of subjectivity, which is the evocation of and externalization of internal moods," he wrote. "Every chord should evoke a particular emotion and you must learn to hear what you play and feel that emotion."

After a few stormy years during which they broke up and then later moved in together, Fahey and Melody decided to tie the knot on November 25, 1978. It would be Fahey's final (and most enduring) marriage. Long since removed from the daily process of record label administration, Fahey, with the help of Denny Bruce, decided to sell off Takoma to Chrysalis Records, who used the label and its catalog to relaunch a more roots-oriented sublabel. "So Chrysalis wanted to do an American roots label and put me in charge," says Bruce. "John's psychiatrist told him not to sell the label, that he needed something on a day-to-day level more than he needed any money. He hung in, and one day he said he was done."

The sale of the label facilitated another major life change, one that he had longed for: to move away from Los Angeles. "The reason that I got rid of [Takoma] was almost everybody in the office started taking cocaine and I couldn't get rid of it," said Fahey. "We weren't losing money or anything. We were still selling records. I made the terrible mistake of giving stock to the employees so I couldn't fire them. The only thing I could do was to dissolve the company. While I was doing that, Chrysalis offered to buy it and I said 'sure, take it." The sale had an immediate positive effect, but the long-term reverberations would last for years.

After the demise of Takoma, he spent more time around the house. Melody, who considered herself eccentric as well, rolled with Fahey's mood swings and occasionally drunken behavior. He tried to hide his drinking from her and indulged to even greater excess in her absence, relieved by the chance to binge without being scolded. "He would go on for periods where he would have a lot of problems with drinking, although he went through periods without drinking too. The sleeping pills he took were chloral hydrate, which he took a lot," remembers Melody.

In their own way, they tried to live like a normal couple, some-times entertaining guests in their home after shows. Michael Chap-man recalls one night in particular, after a show the two played in Los Angeles in 1981. Fahey invited him back to his place afterward. "It was insane," says Chapman. "This was in southeast L.A., where, as Melody said, 'even the dogs bark in Spanish.' It was just my wife and I, John and Melody. John was drinking brandy and Coke, half and half, he was missing a lot and spilling on himself. He offered me a drink and I asked for some white wine, and he reaches into this fridge and pulls out a gallon jug. He asks my wife, who also asks for white wine, and he pulls out another gallon jug for her. I saw quickly where the night was going. At around 2 AM, John is naked at the end of the dinner table except for a genuine Nazi flag from the Nuremberg rallies. He was moaning that Melody wouldn't let him wear his flag to bed. The phone rings at about 3 AM and John just mumbles into the phone and hangs up. We asked who it was and he said it was a journalist asking for an interview that he said was scheduled for right now. Some guy shows up and claims to be some long-lost cousin of John's from Oklahoma. We tried to go to this bar, which had a sign that said 'every beer in the world.' Of course they wouldn't let John in. He had been banned."

Melody became anxious to live in a real house and start a family, while Fahey had simply longed to get farther away from the chaos of society. She gave up her career and the pair relocated to Salem, Oregon, in 1981, where John purchased a modest house for the two of them. They could have afforded something bigger, but modest was what he felt they needed. In private, he seemed scared and conflicted by the move. No longer balanced through yoga, which he had abandoned, his demand as a musician had largely peaked. In a letter to a friend at the time he asked, "You might pray for me. I'd really appreciate it, whether you believe it or not. I am severely depressed right now and feeling suicidal and I don't know why. I have been seeing the shrink that analyzed me. See, I just put down money on a nice house in Salem, Oregon and I should feel excited but I don't feel excited."

Regardless of his reservations, Fahey took to the role of husband and supporter. He battled with his issues but kept Melody close to him. He had ideas about masculinity and the male role as provider in the marriage. "I had a career working in educational films, but once we moved to Oregon he was supporting me completely," says Melody. "If I started to get too independent, sometimes he'd say I was upsetting the balance of power. He liked to be in charge of things." Melody did not complain about the arrangement, and the two tried to settle into their new town. In the summer they went to the local quarry, where Fahey would swim and the two of them would picnic. He practiced his guitar while Melody strummed a few chords on a ukulele. These were good times for the couple.

Fahey often donated money to various charities. Few things gave him more pleasure than seeing a homeless person in a Dumpster and then handing him or her a twenty-dollar bill. His generosity sometimes extended beyond his means. "One year he gave $2,000 to this Catholic charity that was a shelter for runaway kids in New York, and our accountant told me that after all our deductions we only made $11,000 that year," Melody remembers. "He said that John shouldn't give that much to charity, but I couldn't stop him if that's what he wanted to do. I didn't want to stop him."

In the winters, unable to bike, ride, or swim, Fahey grew restless, feeling trapped in the house. He converted the basement into a makeshift studio and record room. Down there, he sought the solace he needed to find inspiration. In preparation for his shows, and to generate new material, he spent hours playing guitar—perhaps heeding his own advice. "If you make yourself play the guitar for four to six hours, I can guarantee that you will come out of these sessions with something new: a composition, an arrangement, a fragment," recommended Fahey in his instructional book. "That is the way the mind works. In order to conquer boredom and chaos, you cannot avoid coming up with something new. I recommend these long sittings rather than short sittings more often per week." In Oregon, he had time to himself to compose, yet he remained consumed by memories of the past. Although he had attained a relative stability in his marriage and career, he soon began to struggle with unresolved issues, memories that became the focus of his remaining years.

LET GO

> "The Void is a term you find in existentialist writers and it's particularly well-described by some Catholic mystics in books on contemplation. It's how you feel when the bottom drops out. It's worse than the blues. Some of the music I've written is a description of this state."
>
> —John Fahey, interview, 1980

Fahey's influence in the 1980s reached new heights when a breed of guitarists who had grown up listening to his records came of age. William Ackerman, an unabashed Fahey acolyte (his first album is titled *In Search of the Turtle's Navel*), founded the acoustic-based record label Windham Hill, which focused on instrumental, meditative music. The music was so light, it hardly seemed there—the type of stuff well suited for dentist waiting rooms, far from the pain of the blues or the experimentalism of modern composers.

Inspired by Fahey's initial vision of instrumental composition for guitar, Ackerman slowly built an empire by marketing the material as New Age, playing perfectly to aging baby boomers who wanted something relaxing to listen to during dinner parties or yoga lessons.

This Muzak sold millions of copies and became the boilerplate for elevator music. Ackerman eventually sold Windham Hill for an estimated $28 million.

Ackerman's own instrumental solo work sold well, but the label found a mass audience with instrumental guitarist Michael Hedges, whose pyrotechnic hammer-on technique packed theaters and dazzled listeners. The associations with Fahey were difficult to avoid. For one, former Takoma artists George Winston and Robbie Băsho released albums for Windham Hill. Fahey's influence over the next generation led to some calling him the father of New Age guitar, a title that offended him like no other. Fahey often called it "hot tub music," seeing it as codified shallowness being done in his name. "He hated those guys," recalls Denny Bruce. "He started being called a New Age guitarist. Just say 'John Fahey' and 'New Age' and he would lose it." It may well have been professional jealousy at the root of his contempt. Windham Hill quickly surpassed Takoma in terms of commercial success.

Fahey openly rejected any notion that his music had anything in common with New Age. He only noticed this connection professionally when his touring schedule booked him with Windham Hill guitarists such as Hedges. The fact that he had discovered George Winston only added fuel to his ire. This association with New Age led him to believe that he had failed as an artist. He got through, getting drunk to escape his discomfort.

He fared much better at home. Steadily performing or recording, he seldom had to do much outside of his interest or scope. He stayed famous as a cult icon to guitarists, new players continually discovering his vast catalog, which provided him with enough cachet to tour and record new albums. As long as he maintained his modest lifestyle, that was all he wanted. "John's main goal in life was never money," Melody says. "He wanted to do certain things. Money was good and it was a good thing to have but he didn't like the idea of having the best of something." Fahey seemed happy in their little house, a Louvin Brothers poster gracing the entrance of his basement lair. Creating new music and developing as an artist remained central to his identity. His desire to propel his music forward and not become stagnant continued to drive him, and his creativity and skill were still completely at his disposal.

Fahey made a pair of records for Chrysalis Records' Takoma, run by Denny Bruce, which had recently enjoyed platinum success with acts like the Fabulous Thunderbirds. *Live in Tasmania*, released in 1981, finds Fahey performing fantastically in front of an enthusiastic audience. However, it isn't really a live record—no surprise considering Fahey's adversarial relationship to the act of live performance. Fahey did indeed perform live in Tasmania, but the tracks on the album are from studio sessions (two songs from his Reprise sessions and perhaps more from a studio session he booked while in Tasmania). The applause was edited in later—another subtle ruse in the Fahey discography. His final album for the label, 1983's *Railroad*, revisits older material, giving them new titles in an attempt to regain some control of his back catalog. Some of his publishing was owned by ex-managers and uninterested parties, so he rerecorded and retitled his pieces in order to use them on new albums. Fans considered the record a spectacular return to form, hearing Fahey perform updated versions of his classic material.

By 1984 Takoma folded, existing only in publishing form; Bruce moved on to other projects. With this, Fahey needed to sell himself in the marketplace of the music industry for the first time, and was completely at the mercy of other labels. Though relieved not to have to deal with the responsibilities of running a business, not having a musical home caused further anxiety for him as he shopped around his recordings. Through his network of intense devotees, Fahey was able to navigate the choppy waters of a free agent.

After leaving Takoma, Fahey started to release records with traditional folk music labels, including Shanachie and Varrick. Shanachie, home to artists like Grateful Dead lyricist David Grisman and world music acts such as the Chieftans, issued his *God, Time and Causality*, while Varrick suggested he record albums with guests—famous friends like George Winston—but plans never got off the ground. Fahey again felt relegated to a musical universe he despised. Yet he always found people who recognized his achievements and championed him, even in the face of a seemingly noncommercial marketplace. One of Fahey's disciples was fingerpicking guitarist Glenn Jones. Jones would go to his shows in Boston, and the two eventually struck up a correspondence and friendship. While working in Rounder distribution as a day job, Jones worked closely with many record labels that released Fahey's albums after Takoma folded.

"Sometimes when you meet someone who's 'famous' they like to talk about themselves and be in that position," remembers Jones. "John talked about himself, I wouldn't say reluctantly, but he was as interested in talking about me. Getting to know John was getting to know yourself better. In some ways he would almost push you into situations where you were uncomfortable talking about yourself. He wasn't doing that to make you uncomfortable but rather as a way to better understand himself—like if you were not always the most popular kid in school, or if you moved around a lot. He was always looking back at his own childhood—girls he had crushes on, kids who beat him, just grade-school social pressures. Getting other people to talk about that stuff was a way to help him figure out his own issues."

John Aloysius Fahey, five and a half
years old. PHOTOGRAPHER UNKNOWN, COURTESY
OF THE COLLECTION OF CHARLIE SCHMIDT

The guitarist as a young man, 1948.
PHOTOGRAPHER UNKNOWN, COURTESY OF THE
COLLECTION OF CHARLIE SCHMIDT

John Fahey, his mother, Jane, and his grandmother Catherine, August 19, 1962, Washington, DC. PHOTOGRAPHER UNKNOWN, COURTESY OF THE COLLECTION OF CHARLIE SCHMIDT

Fahey, September 4, 1962.

PHOTOGRAPHER UNKNOWN, COURTESY OF THE

COLLECTION OF CHARLIE SCHMIDT

Print ad for *Requia*. COURTESY OF
VANGUARD RECORDS, FROM THE COLLECTION
OF GLENN JONES

John and Jan Fahey get close,
November 1967. PHOTOGRAPHER
UNKNOWN, COURTESY OF THE
COLLECTION OF CHARLIE SCHMIDT

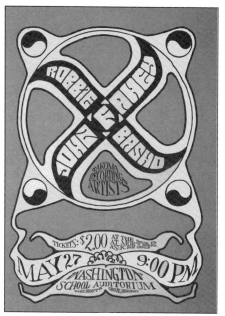

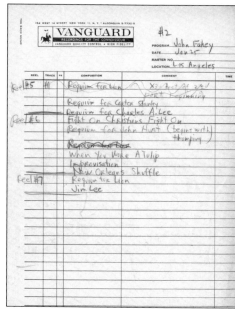

Poster for Takoma artists John
Fahey and Robbie Bāsho, with art
by Tom Weller, 1967. COURTESY OF
THE COLLECTION OF TOM WELLER

Vanguard studio sheet.
COURTESY OF THE COLLECTION
OF SAM CHARTERS

Fahey with tortoise.
PHOTO BY
JOHN VAN HAMERSVELD

Fahey and Denny Bruce, artist
and manager, Hollywood 1971.
PHOTO BY JOHN VAN HAMERSVELD

John and Jan Fahey enjoying a London
vacation, 1969. PHOTOGRAPHER UNKNOWN,
COURTESY OF THE COLLECTION OF JAN LEBOW FAHEY

John and Melody Fahey: happy faces on their wedding day, 1978. COURTESY OF MELODY BRENNAN FAHEY

Fahey's paintings.
COURTESY OF THE
COLLECTION OF BYRON COLEY

Live and electric in Aurora,
Oregon, 1999. PHOTO BY MELISSA
STEPHENSON

Romping with his
animal friends. PHOTOS
BY MELISSA STEPHENSON

Fahey's portrait of Dave Nuss of the No-Neck Blues Band. COURTESY OF DAVE NUSS

Live at the Salem Arts Festival, 1999. PHOTOGRAPHER UNKNOWN, COURTESY OF THE COLLECTION OF MELISSA STEPHENSON

Fahey often got deeply personal with those whom he worked alongside. Having fans entrenched in the industry worked in his favor, but the owners of the labels he recorded for were ultimately interested in the bottom line. His career seemed to stall, with little room for him to move outside his niche. Labels wanted repackaged versions of his Christmas music, the only selling point in his current repertoire in the emerging nostalgia market. They saw him as a folk act, viewing him largely in the context of 1960s music. Fahey still resented the company of what he considered boring contemporaries. Jones recalls one concert that David Grisman and Fahey played together: "We were hanging out backstage. John was headlining, and Grisman was playing, and when John walked backstage past all [Grisman's] friends and hangers-on he had his head down and just muttered 'hate hate hate hate' under his breath, making his vibes known. They got it and they stayed away. The anger was there."

His drinking intensified a crippling depression offstage as well, and the accumulated years of abuse had taken their toll. "He was a very heavy drinker at the time—I would say he was a very serious alcoholic," Jones continues. "He was kind of emotional in the way some alcoholic people are. Anything can set them off. I remember him crying to a Stanley Brothers record in my living room, where the music was affecting him so much he would be weeping uncontrollably. Certainly I think his emotions were very close to the surface, and this was the case throughout when I knew him."

Those close to him knew his struggles; he seldom held back when it came to his personal or professional life. His problems compounded when his health began to fail. But he kept most of his illnesses a mystery, even to his wife. He was unwilling to make lifestyle changes, even in the face of new realities. "He might have been prediabetic and had hypoglycemia; I know he had a lot of problems," remembers

Melody. "He had urinary tract problems for many years and had some operations that were very painful. When you're not feeling well, it's hard to enjoy life."

Still in his forties, he was faced with semiretirement, afflicted with several debilitating medical ailments. For an entire summer he lay bedridden, with no strength to move. The doctors had diagnosed him with the Epstein-Barr virus. The virus manifests itself as mononucleosis in adolescents; when it develops in adults, flulike symptoms and fatigue can persist for months. Fahey's resulting malaise almost drove Melody mad. "For me, it was torture," she remembers. "I don't know what it was like for him. He was in pain and I probably wasn't helping. You think there's nothing wrong with someone and you wonder why they don't get out of bed. But I guess there was something wrong with him. He was tired all the time." Indeed, the symptoms bothered him on and off for several years. Worse, his drinking increased, as he used alcohol to cope with his condition.

In extreme discomfort, he grew insufferable. Unable to work, he lashed out in depressive fits. To further complicate matters, his diet began to spiral uncontrollably. Some remember him eating a gallon of ice cream in one sitting. One friend recalled him ordering a steak and eggs at breakfast, and then another order of steak and eggs to eat in the car on the way back. Glenn Jones recalls him buttering his bacon on more than one occasion. Unsurprisingly, he ballooned in weight, and his hair dangled in long strands around his increasingly balding pate.

Only music kept him engaged and productive. In Portland, he befriended a talented guitarist and arranger named Terry Robb, who was a fan of Fahey's work. After spending a few nights hanging out and trading Charley Patton tunes on guitar, the two formed a close bond. "He was about forty and was just great, and a lot of fun to be around," remembers Robb. "He was really smart. We had a lot of things in common in our likes and dislikes. He would do these crazy things that were hilarious. Every day was filled with some sort of event—like he'd reach into his pocket and pull out a cheeseburger."

Still ready to try new approaches, he expanded his tastes from the blues and bluegrass of his early days. Fahey invited Robb to produce his next record, *Let Go*, a bold step forward. He decided to try his hand at a wide range of material, including even sentimental pop hits like Eric Clapton's "Layla." To Fahey traditionalists, this divergence seemed akin to blasphemy. Always flying in the face of convention, he met the challenge of mainstream rock head on, and tackled the material with sincerity and inventiveness. None of it came naturally to him, so Robb's help was invaluable.

Robb, a lifelong Fahey devotee, admittedly had trouble wrapping his head around the idea at first. "I would try to get him to play like he used to because at the time I was a fan still. He just stopped me and said, 'Look, I'm not doing that anymore. I've already done that. I'm moving on.' Finally I got it, it was like Miles Davis, same thing, moved on. And the thing was, he was up for anything. People always ask about us doing 'Layla' or the Hendrix tune 'May This Be Love.' Some people think I talked him into it, but it was all his idea. He decided he wanted to do those songs, and it was up to me to arrange them."

Robb filled in the blanks, playing many of the backing parts. With Robb, Fahey attempted a more Brazilian feel, even covering his newfound contemporary hero Bola Sete on the title track. Remarkably, the two were able to seamlessly integrate Sete's influence with Fahey's already recognizable style. The resulting album garnered great press and solid sales. Fahey seemed able to adopt the new phrasings and play them his own way, still sounding unique, just as he had done with the blues and bluegrass. The album sounds like Fahey, but boldly heading into new territory, with joy.

Robb proved an invaluable asset on the album, and they set forth working on a follow-up: 1985's *Rain Forests, Oceans and Other Themes*. Also released by Varrick, the album features a similar approach. This time the recording was done in a special setting, according to the album's notes, written in the distant voice of a technical narrator: Cascade Recording Studios in Portland, Oregon, during November and December 1984, and February 1985. This studio was at one time a small church, with a tiny pulpit and choir area at the north end. Though not a breakthrough in terms of sales, its intimate performances, with Robb alongside, made it another distinctive addition to Fahey's catalog.

Robb also frequently stepped in as Fahey struggled to take care of himself, in rough shape both physically and mentally. "He would mix his medications and get out of control and get obsessive about things, and he would drink and take too many pills," remembers Robb. "If something bothered him, that's how he'd deal with it, and he would get out of control in the way that people who do those things get. Melody was there to keep him in check and we got to be close, too. I was close to both of them. He depended on me to keep him in check, too. It got to the point where I was sort of handling him as well. He was fragile and depended on people to take care of him."

The root of Fahey's unhappiness rose to the forefront. He began exploring his childhood to an even more intense degree, with a strong focus on Freudian psychology. He claimed to recall memories from his infancy. During many of his therapy sessions, Fahey began experiencing "repressed memories," products of a now largely discredited psychological theory. In these states he had vivid memories of his father sexually abusing him as a child. He recalled these visions in disturbing detail in his memoirs.

There, Fahey graphically describes being held at gunpoint in his grandfather's room when he was just four. In his accounts of these incidents, his father is portrayed as sadistic and deranged, once tying a noose and describing how he would kill him slowly and watch him die if the boy ever told anyone about the abuse. In these accounts, his mother chose to ignore what happened as a defense mechanism, and Fahey grew a bitter resentment toward her for not interceding. Still the doting mother, she tried her best to help, but he refused to involve her in his life in any way. "I wish you knew what he did to me," he wrote to her in *Bluegrass*. "My father was right, you never did really love me, Mom. Never."

These accounts seem hyperbolic to those who knew both father and son. Ex-wife Jan had met Al on several occasions and doubts Fahey's accounts. "He claimed he was abused, but I don't believe him, because it came at a time when it was a fad to have recovered memories. I think it's another story he made up. His father was a tough character." His childhood friends found the allegations equally surprising. "In his book he makes serious allegations," said Dick Spottswood. "That was nothing that was even remotely spoken about at the time. I think I met his father once only in passing."

Melody questioned whether there was sexual abuse, but she knew there was a lot of pain there. "I'm sure there was a lot of emotional abuse going on, because I stayed a week or two with John's father. He had a sadistic streak, and his mother was one of these people who never wanted to speak about anything unpleasant," she recalls.

In order to deal with these severe "memories," he started to attend a support group for male victims of sexual abuse, a few hours south in Eugene. He drove by himself to get there. He attended another group in Portland, and in order to reclaim part of his tormented childhood, his therapist recommended that he carry a teddy bear with him wherever he went.

The intellectual, funny, and endearing qualities of Fahey stood in stark contrast to his neediness and psychological damage. He became dependent upon others and further separated himself from reality. Robb saw both sides of his personality. "John was a pretty together guy," he says. "The thing that made life difficult for him was his childhood. I think that is the root of it all. I really do. He was very well educated, he was civil, he was very generous to me. I would attribute anything that bothered him to that and his relationship to his father."

As with many aspects of Fahey's life, truth and fiction are difficult to parse. He was prone to making up wild stories about all aspects of his life; it wouldn't be unusual for him to tell a journalist that he had a teenage son or invent other outright lies out of boredom, to toy with the mundane process of being interviewed. His writing revealed a panoramic imagination; the bounds of what he believed often spooled into the irrational. With Fahey's wild imagination and disconnect from reality, it's impossible to arrive at anything conclusive regarding the truth of his scandalous accusations. "John's father was an orphan, from what I heard, and abused in an orphanage, so I guess it's kind of like the sins of the father visited the sons," says Melody. "People get abused and they learn to deal with their life in a certain way and they pass that on. John himself had a certain amount of sadistic tendencies where he'd like to push your buttons."

The childhood trauma he perceived as being real overwhelmed his thoughts and his time; he couldn't seem to escape and became further anxiety ridden. "He was showing up at the studio sometimes just really out of his mind," recalls Robb. "I'd calm him down and get him to listen to last night's mix. That was a good diversion. He appreciated that." Music was the only thing that seemed to help him.

Robb and Fahey continued to work together on a series of albums, until the funding from Varrick began to run out. He revisited his Christmas material, and in 1987 released a record entitled *I Remember Blind Joe Death*, which features a slowed-down Fahey taking on Bill Monroe and Bola Sete songs. The record is the sound of a man losing his abilities. Just a few years prior he had been forging ahead; now he wandered lost in the roots of his own process, the fire gone and a pathetic sadness remaining. His illness had clearly affected his playing. Shadows of his former self peek through in isolated moments, but they are few and far between. He just seemed exhausted. "He got tired of it," says Robb. "He would go on the road by himself or with Melody and he'd get lonely. It's hard work. He was a very intense musician—he put a lot into it. You expose yourself emotionally every night to such an intense level that it takes its toll on you. I could see why he'd want to get away from it."

The final project between Fahey and Robb was an album covering 1950s pop hits like "Sea of Love" and "A Rose and a Baby Ruth," on which he is accompanied by Melody on ukulele. The album features no growth or forward momentum; it is instead a senile look at a romantic past that never existed. Released in 1992, the brilliantly titled *Old Girlfriends and Other Horrible Memories* provides insight into his psychological state at the time. It marks the first time he reveals his interest in the pop music of his childhood, acknowledging that between all the classical music and blues he was in fact influenced by the mainstream culture. Though genuinely interested in the oldies material performed on the record, he had neither the capability nor imagination to channel it into something new. The album seems foggy and nostalgic.

His dismissal of his early work remained a constant. "I got interested in '50s rock and roll music and started arranging songs like
'Blueberry Hill' for solo guitar—and mood songs about people and
places where I grew up," Fahey said about the project. "At shows these
days I play almost nothing but '50s music and blues. No longer do
I play long, neo-Wagnerian, pretentious, pompous songs like 'Mark
1:15.' I did quite a few of those disgustingly eclectic, preposterous tone
poems." In truth, he couldn't play intense fingerpicking songs even if
he wanted to.

He also wanted to distance himself from the 1960s and New Age.
The album seems a sentimental hodgepodge, played at half speed, like
an old man crossing a busy road. The only evidence of the old prankster Fahey is found with the uncredited appearance of an Al Wilson
recording, which Fahey titled "Fear & Loathing at 4th & Butternut"
in tribute to his old friend. The recording is an old Takoma session for
a proposed Al Wilson solo album that never came to fruition. It is the
sole nod to his post-Maryland life, and a bittersweet highlight to an
otherwise unremarkable album.

The material provided another reason for Fahey to revisit his
past. The ubiquitous nature of pop radio ensured that these songs
had become part of his subconscious. His preteen romantic experiences suffered none of the realities of his adult relationships, so they
remained a pristine ideal. While on tours, he would go to phone
booths and randomly search for girls from his childhood. Melody
knew about his pattern of behavior and understood that he was really
looking for some sort of closure with his traumatic past, not trying
to ignite an extramarital fling. Sometimes she even helped him look.
"It drove me nuts!" she admits. "One of the things we used to do
when we were on the road was stop at phone booths and try to find
this little girl that he knew when he was a kid that he met at some

campground and just look to see if she was in that phone book," she remembers. "So he'd look in these phone books because maybe her family moved to *this* town." He once even hired a private detective to track down one girl, whom he hadn't spoken to in forty years. When he found her, he was disappointed that she had gotten old and fat, just like him. In his imagination, she remained a perfect distillation of the innocence he imagined he lost in his youth. His expectations were beyond unrealistic, of course, but he ended up moping as a result.

Things at home worsened. Melody had always wanted children, and even though Fahey seemed uninterested in parenting from the beginning, the issue began to cause strain. His constant focus on his childhood caused resentment and unhappiness in the marriage. With nothing else to focus on and no other presence in the home, Melody felt alone. "I don't know if I would have been that great of a mother or if that would have been the end of the marriage, but it didn't happen and I had some anger about that," she says. "John was not quite upfront about that at the beginning. I should have been more realistic about him. You know how people are. When we got married I got this set of crystal, and we never entertained. You have different ideas of what your life is going to turn out like and you find out that it's not really what you want."

With his mounting health problems and their growing discontent, things were looking darker than ever. His playing had deteriorated from lack of practice and he neglected his performing schedule. Aside from some local gigs, the only money coming in was from his publishing and royalty statements, just enough to sustain them. "Jobs would come and he would do them," Melody remembers. "He always had some work. It would just be fairly local, but there was never six months where he didn't have any jobs at all. He did have some guitar students, although that was never his big thing. He had one little boy who was a child of a friend of ours. He introduced him at a concert at the university here, and he was really young and he played one song with John and it was really touching."

His life seemed to have come to a standstill.

Confused and depressed, he decided to make a bold decision. In 1992, Melody was unexpectedly served with divorce papers. There was no precipitating event; Melody had only vague reasons as to why he decided to get a divorce after fifteen years of marriage. He never talked to her directly until after the lawyers got involved, and by then it was far too late to have a civil discussion. After the many years she spent taking care of him, he suddenly cut off all communication with her. So, spurned by him, Melody placed an injunction against him for two years after the divorce. She felt betrayed and angry. "I didn't want to have to fight with him about anything. I didn't want to talk to him at all because I was so upset. Eventually we became friends again, but that's how the divorce went. I got the house and I didn't ask for interest in any of the properties he created during the fifteen years we were married."

In retrospect, Melody felt that perhaps things ended up for the best. "I didn't leave John. John left me," she says. "Later, he said he thought he made a mistake, but it might have been a good thing for me because I would have been stuck with John in his terrible health and it would have been a financial disaster for me. Maybe he was doing me a mitzvah. For instance, with the divorce he once said to me, however mysteriously, that he didn't want to become a monster. He was talking about his physical problems. That might have been part of why he started the divorce—to release me. I never would have divorced him. Having stayed together would have been quite a disaster for me. The way it worked out, I have the house unencumbered. Who knows? It's hard to say what went on. He may have had mixed feelings about me. Sometimes he may have hated me and sometimes he may have thought I was the best thing to ever happen to him. Aren't we all that way?"

Left to his own devices for the first time in many years, Fahey began living in week-to-week motels around Salem. He began writing long essays about his childhood and his experiences as a musician—much in the style of his liner notes. He detailed his ideas, stories, and fantasies, creating a universe through his own filter. In his mind was a world he connected with, and he began trying to translate it to the page.

But there were more banal concerns. He couldn't pick up after himself and became unable to do daily chores. As the day-to-day eluded him further, he retreated into a hermetic existence. Pizza boxes and delivery containers littered his room. He spent his time wandering the streets, haunting the local record stores searching for classical records and drinking. There was little left for him personally or professionally.

Strangely, though, a resurrection waited around the corner. While the folkies were either dead or playing dinner theaters, a new generation of music listeners found his work and began to celebrate it anew.

WHEN THE SPRINGTIME COMES AGAIN

"This new group is all for freedom. That's one hell of an improvement. With the alternative people, there are some social dos and don'ts. But in comparison, it shows that the hippie movement was always quite rigid even though it was always talking about freedom. It was phony."

—John Fahey, interview, 1997

In the 1990s the mainstream music world went through a drastic paradigm shift. The charts had been dominated for decades by manufactured pop stars and larger-than-life rock bands. But success had reached a new breed of musicians, ones groomed on the fringes of record stores, not seeking stardom but driven by an expression of suffering and existential angst. The troubled, tortured artist, best personified by Nirvana front man Kurt Cobain, came to the forefront. Psychology, addiction, and the pathos of the suburbs all became prevalent themes in popular culture. The signifiers of rock stars and their inherent clichés were scuttled. Younger audiences searched for even more obscurities as their alternative heroes name-checked everything from Krautrock to Japanese noise bands. With the rise of Nirvana and other grunge bands, the cult hero had more marketplace cachet than ever.

Record labels, unsure of the boundaries, scrambled to sign up any act that seemed to possess an authentic alternative credibility. Taste-makers became de-facto major-label A&R reps: Sonic Youth's Thurston Moore was responsible for Nirvana's signing to Geffen Records, which resulted in tens of millions of albums sold. As a result, huge checks were cut to almost any band or musician endorsed by Cobain or Moore, from the Meat Puppets to the Boredoms. Bands who a year or two earlier were barely a blip on the radar all of a sudden had major-label record deals.

Similarly, those musicians who had influenced these contemporary successes were given the revival treatment. The more obscure or difficult the musical reference, the greater the appeal for the truly in-the-know. Roky Erickson of the 13th Floor Elevators was brought back—although he was damaged from years of LSD abuse and his time in mental institutions. Daniel Johnston, a severe schizophrenic and manic-depressive who recorded and lived at his mother's house, was signed to a reported seven-figure deal with Atlantic Records after Cobain famously wore a T-shirt Johnston drew while accepting an MTV Video Music Award. Seemingly overnight, being a severely damaged musician was extremely lucrative.

Fahey fit comfortably within this new canon. His discography was already filled with images of death, rejection, and lost loves. To a bummer generation, Fahey provided a perfect soundtrack. Much like at the 1964 Newport Folk Festival, forgotten recluses were being brought out years later for their moment of cultural appreciation.

Rhino Records issued a double-CD set of the best of John Fahey. Compiled by old buddy Barry Hansen, the album was titled, at Fahey's insistence, *Return of the Repressed*. "I spent a day with him in Salem to work on *Return of the Repressed*," says Hansen. "As others have stated, he was living in a 'welfare motel.' The room was piled high with LPs that he had gleaned from local thrift shops. He supported himself by selling the better ones to affluent collectors around the country, very much a 1990s analog to what he had done in the 1960s with blues 78s."

Released in 1994, this set introduced Fahey's music to the digital age and included tracks from most of his 1960s and '70s Takoma records. The material sounded fresh and exciting to modern listeners. He seemed adamant about not being part of some hippie nostalgia trip. However, feeling as though he never fit into the image of 1960s rock 'n' roll culture, he remained wary about his old work being reintroduced. Fahey had already disassociated himself from the American Primitive fingerpicking style with which he had become synonymous. "I was writing these things as an escape, as a possible way to make money," he claimed. "The sentiments expressed come out of a fucked up situation. I was creating for myself an imaginary, beautiful world and pretending that I lived there, but I didn't feel beautiful. I was mad but I wasn't aware of it. I was also very sad, afraid and lonely. By presenting this so-called beautiful facade I looked good to myself and to my audience." Luckily, Hansen took care of writing the notes.

When Fahey couldn't afford his weekly fleabag motel he took shelter at the Union Gospel Mission across Salem, the only place left for him to go. The mission was often filled with drug dealers and other unsavory people. Fahey would find cocaine bags stashed behind the toilets and was once mugged while staying there. But more objectionable to Fahey than the criminal element was the mission's dogmatic interpretation of Christianity, which the staff demanded from those who entered. For Fahey, it was one of the most difficult conditions of staying there. Forced to attend meetings and discuss one-sided views of theology, he became increasingly frustrated at having to accept their version of religion in order to keep his bed. If he did not regurgitate the ethos preached therein they cast him out and he slept in his car. So he bit his tongue and played by the rules.

Fahey became so removed from society and his former life that few knew how dire his living situation was. "I didn't know when he moved to Salem, so that's how much we kept in touch," says former manager Denny Bruce. "We had the same CPA, and one day I got a call from him asking me to come see him because John needed a check FedExed to him right away, as he was in very bad shape. Our share of some Kottke check was $120 each. I had no idea what he was going to do with it until I saw it was addressed to John Fahey, care of the Salvation Army. I was shocked. That was the first time I heard."

Even those who knew about his living conditions felt that perhaps it had been his choice to live in squalor. "John did spend quite a bit of time creating his own myths, and I think maybe the Union Gospel Mission was part of that, the myth of John Fahey," says Melody.

Within the music industry, new myths were being written about Fahey, too—ones that seemed to understand his perspective as part of a pantheon of American independent artists. Music critic Byron Coley wrote for and coedited one of the decade's most beloved underground magazines, *Forced Exposure*. Known for his expertise in the outsider and the difficult, Coley had long followed Fahey's career. "When I started hanging out with Glenn Jones, we each had people who we were obsessed with collecting, and Fahey was one of his," recalls Coley. After Jones explained Fahey's significance, Coley fully understood the bigger picture. "We were into people like Sun Ra, Harry Partch, Michael Hurley. There was a pantheon of people who put out their own records and ran their own labels. From that point on, with the people who I hung out with, Fahey was one of the pantheon."

Through Jones, Coley learned that Fahey had fallen on hard times. He pitched an idea to *Spin* magazine: he would get the story on the current whereabouts and activities of this reclusive genius guitar player if they would fund the trip to Salem. "People were buying the records and people assumed he was dead," Coley adds. "It led to the obvious comparison of people thinking blues guys are dead." The parallels to Fahey's own discovery of Skip James were striking. In turn, Fahey himself became the keeper of lost secrets from the past; he seemed as alien to the alternative crowd as James had been to the folk revivalists.

Fahey, living in a flophouse in Salem, was an ideal candidate for rediscovery. When Coley went to see him, he was immediately caught off guard. Fahey opened the door with his robe wide open, naked underneath. His room was covered with pizza boxes and takeout containers; piles of records and books were strewn about haphazardly. After Coley explained why he was there, Fahey told him to leave, saying he felt tired. When Coley returned the next day and told him he spent the previous day shopping at record stores, Fahey got excited. The two spent the next few days driving to every record store in Oregon, and ate plenty along the way. Fahey was overjoyed by eating and shopping on someone else's dime.

"He was hilarious," recalls Coley. "He was so mean. He would say the meanest shit about people. I would ask him about this stuff, like what was the deal on *Fare Forward Voyagers*. He was really into this girl, the secretary Shanti Norris who was the maharishi's secretary at the ashram in L.A., and thought if he did the record maybe she would go out with him. I thought it was so fucked up. He said the worst thing about living in his town was all the Mormon broads. One day a Mormon woman came to his door on her mission or whatever and she's talking to him and he thinks she's really cute. So he gets the Book of Mormon and reads it and tells her it's a piece of shit and that he couldn't believe anyone could believe in that. He would ramble on endlessly about the weirdest shit."

Coley got the impression that Fahey was well known around town and often a difficult presence. Few people around him were sufficiently well versed in Fahey's obscure interests to have a meaningful conversation with him.

The subsequent feature, which ran in *Spin* in 1994, introduced Fahey to a new, younger audience. As presented by Coley, Fahey seems equally charming and troubled, but his intelligence comes across perfectly. Seeing the world through his own lens, he was a perfect feature subject for an alternative music culture. Having been endorsed by the rock heroes of the day, Fahey was seen by younger fans as a precursor to the contemporary movement rather than a relic of their parents' generation like the Grateful Dead or James Taylor. Fahey was branded an authentic outsider genius and suddenly there was renewed interest in his work.

For the first time Fahey embraced his audience and felt generally excited about the people who were interested in his music. "In the current season, the only people who understand me and with whom I have anything in common are punks and alternatives and industrial and no wave and anti-folk, etc." Fahey said. "Last year there was a big spread on me in *Spin* by Byron Coley. *Spin*, not some damned folk music zine or new age yoga yuppie magazine. My category is alternative, period. I object to another categorization. Of course, the matter is out of my hands and I cannot prevent you from doing whatever you want to do, but I want to tell you how I—just in case you are interested—look and feel about these matters," wrote Fahey in a letter to Fantasy Records, the company that owned and reissued his earlier Takoma catalog on compact disc.

His day-to-day reality still lacked cohesion as he stumbled around town seeking solace. Lonely and lacking company, he talked to anyone who shared his interests. He relied on his ability to scavenge records, the one skill that he constantly maintained a grasp on. However, he became a burden to the local record stores and their staff, often putting records on hold that he couldn't pay for and generally being a nuisance. "A few record store guys in Salem knew who he was, but I had the feeling he could be a real pain in the ass in these places," remembers Coley. "He seemed to know a lot of people around town, but I can't imagine many of them knew what he was talking about most of the time." One record store clerk found Fahey sitting on the corner after the store had closed, sobbing. The owner had reshelved the records Fahey had on hold but couldn't afford.

Fahey had finally achieved the isolation he claimed to crave, but it came at a cost. His grip on reality was worsening. Left to his own devices, he had little motivation to interact with the outside world— until he discovered the last few decades of experimental music. While Fahey had been aware of experimental composers like John Cage in the 1960s, he was completely unaware of the decades of abstract music that had been made subsequently, from nihilist punk to noise music. Fahey loved the idea of being part of the continuum of artists whose work lay outside the folk or rock worlds. These audiences weren't interested in people like Leo Kottke or the technical guitarists or the New Age lightness of Windham Hill. The bold despair and radicalism in Fahey's work had finally been manifested elsewhere.

Coley would often get late-night phone calls from Fahey, who harangued him on a multitude of subjects. Coley witnessed Fahey's eccentricities far beyond the writing of the article. "I stayed in touch with him, and sometimes he'd be really funny and super pissed off," recalls Coley. "He was angry that I hadn't told him about industrial music. He was mad because I knew all this stuff about this experimental music and I hadn't told him. He was obviously off his rocker a little bit."

New opportunities and unparalleled resources emerged. Coley teamed up with Geffen Records executive and former SST Records employee Ray Farrell to sign Fahey to Geffen for a six-figure check. The plan was for him to rerecord the Fonotone material, which at that time was only six sides, with Sonic Youth as his backing band and platinum-selling Geffen star Beck singing vocals. It seemed to them a sweet deal for the down-on-his-luck musician. Fahey didn't have to do much of anything, and he could collect a check large enough to keep him living comfortably in his old age.

Contracts were drawn up, but Fahey turned the deal down, saying that he didn't find the idea interesting. "I got the impression that he just refused to do anything that someone else suggested, regardless of what their intention was," says Coley. "He was able to negate that [concept], as it didn't spring from him." In truth, creating music was not a priority for him. He didn't even own a guitar then, and showed little interest in playing.

Fahey's recent press had brought a new batch of supporters to help revive his career. One reader affected by his story was Dean Blackwood, a twenty-five-year-old lawyer and record collector. Blackwood had recently started the label Perfect Records, dedicated to making 78 RPM records, a format as obscure and difficult as the music he chose to release. Having recently issued a 78 by the outsider/improv/jazz band

Sun City Girls, he reached out to Fahey to see if he was interested in recording something for his label. Immediately, Blackwood saw that Fahey desperately needed assistance and decided to take on the task of helping Fahey with his various problems. Most urgently, several collection agencies were after him for old debts, which had been steadily accruing interest while he ignored them. His only income was from the marginal payments he got on his publishing.

These publishing companies were controlled by legendary folk manager Manny Greenhill for many years, and his son Mitch took over after he died. "All Fahey's own records, the underlying compositions were published by [Manny Greenhill's] companies," says Blackwood. "All his sales and mechanical royalties, all Kottke's, all the Takoma stuff was collected there even though [Fahey] sold the master recordings many years ago. He still retained the publishing for Kottke and Băsho. I don't know if that extended to everyone on the label but at least the Fahey and Kottke stuff. There was a little nest egg there. We were forced to draw on it periodically to keep the lights on, literally. He always had some situation and needed money wired to him and that was how it worked with Mitch. He'd just get a call when he needed money."

This royalty income was the only thing separating him from complete ruin. With proper management, Blackwood believed Fahey could regain some sense of normalcy. He offered to manage Fahey and began to put his various affairs in order, initially thinking the weekly motels were the root of the problem. "I remember working out the math at the time. The motels were four times what it would be for an apartment—and a nice place, too," says Blackwood. "The services at a motel offered him certain freedoms from ordinary hygiene, which was important, I would come to find out. Initially after doing this analysis I thought that getting him out of the motels was crucial in order to get him back on track. He needed someone to mind a budget and whatnot. I learned after working with him for a while that there was a disproportional value in the economics of the thing and it in fact did make sense to have someone there to sort of hover over him in the background and make sure he didn't disappear in a sea of pizza boxes."

Blackwood arrived at a crucial time. Without a wife to anchor him emotionally, Fahey had lost himself. "When you operate in that kind of world for several decades, the condition probably transcends will," says Blackwood. "He was no longer capable. Looking at a bill that had been slipped under the door and being able to pay it, I think he lost the capacity to do that over years of dedicating himself against doing so. It wasn't just him being a lifelong contrarian, which he was in spades. It had become a true dysfunctional aspect of his personality. In that sense he really was an outsider."

With Blackwood on board as his legal aide and manager, Fahey wanted to get back to focusing on his creative endeavors. He dreamed of being truly independent, and had an endless stream of ideas. This too was a fantasy, however, as he needed others to take care of him. "He wasn't the kind of artist that could build a cabin in the woods and sustain himself outside of society," adds Blackwood. "He had needs that could only be satisfied by us here in the modern world."

Then came an unexpected turning point. In 1995, Fahey's estranged father passed away. He had lived the rest of his life in the house on New York Avenue in Takoma Park, where John had lived as a young boy. An NRA member, Al had amassed a cache of loaded guns, which were found at the time of his death, and the house surrounded by barbed wire. He had also amassed a considerable amount of money. And, to everyone's surprise, he left it to his only son. It was enough for John to pay his creditors, and then some.

Fahey decided the best course of action with the remainder of the inheritance was to start a new record label. He partnered with Blackwood to handle the back end. With a more adventurous audience tuned into his music, Fahey curated a dream label of his favorite artists, while Blackwood introduced more contemporary acts. "Our initial conversations were more just general musings about record labels and what was wrong with them, and what was right with some of them," Blackwood says. "And wouldn't it be great if someone focused on these neglected artists? And what if people took these luxurious cocoons of packaging combined with the beauty of the sounds?"

Blackwood and Fahey's plan was to repackage and present both old and new material at the aesthetic heights they felt it deserved. They decided to name their new label Revenant Records and quickly began working on projects with new artists and reissues of Fahey favorites like the Stanley Brothers. Younger audiences who had already found Fahey were curious about roots as well as contemporary music. By making highly detailed reissue sets they figured they could appeal to new collectors who could see the Revenant catalog as a viable way to approach outsider American music. "They were appreciative of art and design being married with these gorgeous sounds, so it seemed like there was an opportunity to tap into, if only someone had the money to do it," says Blackwood. "So when the money came, we had been talking about Dock Boggs and Charley Patton and early Stanley Brothers and Ornette Coleman."

Blackwood's legal background was crucial in negotiating the murky waters of music from decades past. "A lot of the legality was in a gray area," says Blackwood. "At the time there was a possibility that stuff from at least as far back as the '20s could still not be technically public domain, depending on what the copyright holders had done." Major labels didn't seem too intent on searching their legal agreements from decades earlier for the obscure artists Revenant sought to put out, so the new albums went to market unopposed.

Featuring extensive notes and critical analysis, Revenant's releases were a treasure trove of folk and blues for collectors. The culmination of its approach was the release of the previously unissued fourth volume of Harry Smith's iconic *Anthology of American Folk Music*. Packaged with a level of detail that satisfied the most hardcore collector, the two-disc set served as a stunning addendum to America's most definitive and long-standing compilation of folk music.

Revenant became an immediate success, and their roster quickly expanded to include formidable contemporary acts such as Jim O'Rourke, Sir Richard Bishop, and the Bassholes. These artists not only gave the label a modern voice but also highlighted the lineage of Fahey's influence. If Fahey had absorbed the influences of his youth and recontextualized them, many of Revenant's contemporary artists had achieved their own innovations using Fahey as an influence. Younger artists were happy to work with Revenant; Fahey's iconoclast persona helped seal the deal, even if he rarely interacted with the artists themselves. Revenant not only gave Fahey a modern context as an influence on the new school of guitar innovators, but also reestablished him as a cultural tastemaker, exhibiting his curatorial expertise and fanatical dedication. Blackwood handled the day-to-day aspects of the operation from his home in Tennessee. They stayed in close contact, and Blackwood did the best he could to keep Fahey's and Revenant's affairs in order.

Apart from standard albums, the label also became known for their elaborate box sets of twentieth-century outsider musicians. Free jazz saxophone legend Albert Ayler and abstract blues-rock kings Captain Beefheart & the Magic Band both received the full Revenant box set treatment: packaged in beautifully designed boxes, and filled with unreleased tracks, images, and detailed historical liner notes. Both Ayler's nine-disc box and Beefheart's five-disc set garnered praise and sales, though very little money was to be made.

New difficulties set in when Fahey and Blackwood worked with established living artists. It was hard sometimes penetrating the mindsets of artists who came of musical age in the 1960s and had existed on the fringe of commercial recording companies, like Beefheart and Ayler. Blackwood explains, "None of them ever got paid in the day, so they see a big project as evidence of several things: one, that they will finally get paid; two, you wouldn't be interested in doing the project unless you were going to get paid; and three, that by definition a large project has a large audience. None of those things were true in most cases. The types of projects we put out were extensive. It's hard to tap into the uninitiated. We tried to appeal to both the hardcore fan base and to those who were just more adventurous in their music listening and might try something extensive if it was done very well and had a great presentation. In the end, at most, for your highest-sales-potential item, you get maybe in the low tens or twenty thousand copies worldwide over a period of time."

After recouping the substantial expense of the elaborate production costs and then splitting up the proceeds between the various artists and publishers, there was little profit. However, the quality of Revenant's releases garnered instant appreciation from its niche public, and it quickly solidified the label's merit. What's more, it furthered Fahey's legendary status. *Spin* named Revenant's *Captain Beefheart & His Magic Band Grow Fins* best reissue of 1999, and it received four stars in *Rolling Stone*. The *Chicago Tribune* called the Albert Ayler *Holy Ghost* set "the Everest of all jazz boxed sets of 2004. . . . A major event. . . . 'Holy Ghost' represents a long overdue restoration of Ayler's art to a listening public that has had scant chance to hear it."

Unsurprisingly, the Revenant project closest to Fahey's heart had to be the Charley Patton seven-CD box set *Screamin' and Hollerin' the Blues: The Worlds of Charley Patton*. The set included all of Patton's existing recordings, as well as a slew of music that was influenced by him, setting up Patton as a legend in his own right. "There was a sense that there was really something to tap into because there hadn't been anything like that since the Robert Johnson set," says Blackwood.

Also included in the Patton set was a reprinted and reworked edition of Fahey's thesis on Patton, which had originally been published in Europe in the early 1970s. In addition to his own research, Fahey reached out to his old friend Dick Spottswood for assistance with the set. The mighty box set became the ultimate collection of Patton research and ephemera. So impressive was the production value that Revenant earned three Grammys, for Best Historical Album, Best Box or Special Limited Edition Package, and Best Album Notes. Being the foremost expert on Charley Patton garnered Fahey industry-wide recognition. Fahey was indeed a serious musicologist, a man who knew about traditional American music, in addition to being a record collector and musician of stature.

In the fifth decade of his musical career, Fahey had reached a new high. His own music, however, found a more mixed reception.

DANCE OF THE INHABITANTS

"I'm just doing solo electric. One gets old, and then the fingers hurt. I mean I've got an acoustic, but Jesus, it kills me. Like razor blades cutting into my left fingers. Then I can't practice the next day. I tend to do very long practicing, like for hours, and I just can't do it. Life is so tough."

—John Fahey, interview, 2000

If Fahey intended for his music to be the conduit for his negative emotions, the current climate of music basically begged for little else. Fahey's love affair with the modern, experimental guitarists was a two-way street. Seeing the complete absence of the politics or sentimentality characteristic of the folkies, hippies, or New Agers, he embraced his new stylistic freedom with abandon.

Fahey had heard a record of the prepared guitar work of experimental musician Jim O'Rourke. Musically, O'Rourke's records at the time were abstract and minimal, using the guitar as a sound source rather than traditional picking or strumming, and eschewing any traditional forms or structures. Having grown up with a strict

midwestern background, the overtly polite improviser became a perfect foil for the notoriously difficult Fahey.

O'Rourke's interest in music straddled both the improvisational
and the compositional, and he had created a staggering body of work
by his midtwenties. He was influenced strongly by both Fahey and
by minimalist composers like Tony Conrad, which informed his
broad musical template. O'Rourke was in high demand as a producer
and collaborator, working with the likes of Faust and Henry Kaiser,
among others. His musical prowess gave him the ability to help translate even the most difficult and abstract musical ideas.

Unlike most other guitarists whom Fahey encountered, O'Rourke
had little interest in either the technical aspects of guitar playing or its
bluesmen. Fahey, impressed by O'Rourke's extreme guitar manipula-
tions, found his phone number and called him out of the blue, asking him to help on new recordings. Stunned by the call, O'Rourke
initially thought it a practical joke. He never imagined that Fahey
listened to his work. The two eventually met in Los Angeles, where
O'Rourke was working with former Fahey associates the Red Krayola. "Fahey isn't an Americana thing for me, although I understand
that it's really the roots of the music," says O'Rourke. "But it's this
other part, the minimalist aspect that he tapped into, that was really
important to me. I don't think he knew what the hell I was talking
about, but he understood that I didn't think of him in the context of
Bukka White. I didn't give a shit about that stuff, honestly."

Inspired by the experimental music community, Fahey grew
bolder in his own approaches. No longer focused solely on music, he
began to explore other outlets of expression and creative release. His
fascination with his past demanded further exploration. The results
filled notebooks, with stories of friends, childhood, and career all getting equal treatment. The occasionally lucid accounts of his career

were offset by the descriptions of the wild fantasy world of Takoma Park. Though unreliable as a narrator, as an author of fiction he came across as both wildly entertaining and emotive. Fahey also displayed his sentimental side, detailing his childhood crushes and fantasy loves. In one such description of a teenage love, he wrote, "Yes, I wonder what would have happened if I hadn't gone for a walk that balmy day in April. Whatever would have happened I'm glad it didn't. As far as I can see or feel, Dianne turned out to be my salvation. The girl I met that solstice spring day when she utterly destroyed my unconscious vow to remain superficial, unconnected, cold—that's why I had been afraid of the winter. I had been afraid of myself. But she wasn't afraid of me. Not my beloved tassel time girl."

But the true shock lay in the vivid depictions of sexual abuse committed by his father. One particular scene tells of his father showing him what would happen if he told anyone about the abuse: "He made a noose out of the sash pull hanging down from the ceiling," Fahey wrote. "He made it very slowly and looped end around end. And while he did this he told me what it was like to die by hanging. How I would gag and gasp for breath but wouldn't die because he wouldn't let me die by breaking my neck. Oh no. That would be too easy and too quick. He wanted me to strangle and strangle for a long time."

Blurred together, the material made for fascinating reading and eventually found a publisher at the Drag City record label, home to Jim O'Rourke and largely thanks to his efforts. Fahey had pulled them out of the trash at O'Rourke's insistence. "He told me about the writing in one of our first conversations, before the record or any of that," recalls O'Rourke. "We started talking about movies and he told me how he punched out Antonioni once. He told me he wrote a story about it and that he would send it to me. The next day I got a box FedExed to me full of pages and stories that were stained in spaghetti

sauce and just a mess. That was the first book." Once they were collected and edited, under the title *How Bluegrass Music Destroyed My
Life*, Fahey had something of a fictional memoir. Fiction and reality
had always held little distinction for the author, so readers were left to
decide for themselves the stories' veracity.

The life and times of Fahey, although presented in a highly sub-
jective fashion, left plenty for audiences to pore over. Besides his traumas, he presented his take on Skip James, folk festivals, Antonioni,
young love, and patience—all in his unmistakable narrative voice.
The book became a success for all parties, selling more than ten thousand copies. More important, it further perpetuated the John Fahey
mythos. As a young man he had sought answers regarding life's great
questions from the elder bluesmen he encountered. He in turn was
imparting his own sage wisdom to a new generation via his memoirs.

His creative outlets were widening. He took up whole new avenues
of expression, including painting. He created abstracts with water-
colors and spray paint, sometimes in deep traditional colors, other
times with bright neon. The painting seemed a direct reflection of his
moods, sometimes splattered across the paper, other times drowned in
ink and textured by diffusion. The bold colors and blotchy shapes are
reminiscent of Rorschach tests. He'd make dozens of pieces at a time,
transforming his motel rooms into paint-splattered studios, much to
the dismay of the cleaning staffs and management. "John's life was
his work," remembers Melody. "Maybe I inspired him somewhat with
painting. After we split up, I was making a living buying and selling
things at yard sales and estate sales. John asked me if I could get him
some powdered paint. He made these small paintings by putting the
powder in wet phone books and then he'd stomp on them; then he'd
sell them for five dollars at his shows." He also mailed packages of
several dozen to Byron Coley, unbidden, for him to sell at record fairs.

"He asked me to sell them for $10 apiece, and asked me to wire him $300, which is ridiculous because it costs $50 to wire something. He made me send it to some Western Union in Salem," says Coley. "Then he asked me how they were selling and I said I sold a few. Then the next time he'd say, 'You know you really got to give me more money for those paintings' and I just said I only made $40 so far. Then he'd send me some more. I had so many of them."

His return to music was equally nontraditional. Fahey committed acoustic heresy and switched for the first time ever to electric guitar. In this new medium he played exploratory, extended, improvised material. The music sounds distant, covered in reverb. His playing seems slow, as if each note were the result of great effort. The rich melodies and virtuosity that attracted his original fans is largely absent, leaving the skeletal elements of his signature style adrift in a pool of effects. Rather than attempting elaborate compositions, he repeats elementary refrains in a stilted, hesitant manner. It sounds as if he is relearning the instrument after not playing for many years. Even so, he finally felt free to pursue the edges of his playing with little thought of technique, melody, or audience.

With few expectations, he released his first album of new music in years, 1997's *City of Refuge*, on Tim/Kerr Records. The album title is another reference to his troubled relationship with his parents. He explained:

> It was a place my parents took me to when I was a child. It was along the Atlantic Ocean somewhere, and we ran out of food and water and we went into this mysterious city. It was just so weird. There were no people, but there was a big factory. I had a recurrent dream about it that my parents had planned to take me to the city to chop me up and consume me. But the factory communicated with me and warned me what they were planning, and me and the factory consumed my parents instead.

Fahey, still lost in the throes of repressed memories, produced a mixed bag of noise collages, meandering electric and acoustic guitar, and various sampled sounds. Elements of his original style can be heard, but they are juxtaposed with colder electronic sounds. There was little to comfort fans of his vintage 1960s acoustic work. The innovations of the last several decades were new and exciting to Fahey, but for those who had been listening to experimental music, Fahey's new direction lacked cohesion, as if he were being difficult for the sake of it.

Even ardent supporters had nothing good to say about the album. Glenn Jones wrote:

> Little of *City of Refuge* can be considered groundbreaking, whether in light of the works of '80s and '90s sampling artists; the overwhelming (and largely undifferentiated) bulk of industrial music created in the wake of Throbbing Gristle and SPK in the late '70s; the musical anarchism of the '60s art-rock; the Fluxus and futurist composers; the works of electronic and musique concrete composers in the '40s, '50s and '60s, the dada and noise composers of the '20s—or by Fahey's own previous high-water mark.

He continues with a sentiment that many shared about the tepid album's slow crawl: *"City of Refuge* hasn't shocked old fans so much as it's bored or disappointed many of them. It pales in comparison with most of John's back catalogue, and I believe that if *City of Refuge* were John Fahey's first record, instead of his 40th, it would have gone largely unnoticed."

Jones had spent most of the 1990s playing guitar in the psychedelic band Cul de Sac, a band that aimed to fuse elements of American Primitive, Krautrock, and other disparate influences. As a band of record collectors, Cul de Sac had dreams of collaborating with some of their influences. Jones's longtime correspondence with Fahey made him an ideal potential collaborator, especially now that Fahey had gone electric. Jones suggested that Fahey join his band Cul de Sac for a fleshed-out take on each other's songs. The record label Thirsty Ear agreed to foot the bill for the recording sessions. Fahey and the band rehearsed for ten days in preparation. At the last moment the studio canceled due to lack of payment, and Jones scrambled to find a place to record. Jones recalls the process in the album notes:

> After a Boston photo shoot, we made our way to Warren, Rhode Island's Normandy Studios, the new site for the project. We had nine days to record and mix an album. But after two days of recording basics, John, growing more and more impatient, rebelled. I discovered that he had no interest in making the kind of record I'd envisioned. He attacked the material, said it would be disastrous for his career to be associated with it, and called us a 'retro lounge act.' And while Cul de Sac might run through a song three or four times, Fahey rarely played a song more than once. He has little patience in striving for the perfect take. Accidents and serendipity delight him. I can still see him stretched out on the floor of the studio control room listening to the playback of this album's final track, roaring with laughter.

Whereas Jones had a vision for the album and tried to articulate it, Fahey decided at some point the material was too musical and rebelled, refusing to be involved with it any longer. Jones found working with Fahey a difficult process, despite their years of friendship. "Having been so closely involved with Fahey throughout the project and having had to bear much of the brunt of his claims, I have discovered that John exaggerates or invents things in order to appear in the best possible light," wrote Jones. "He seems willing to change his tune depending on how 'hip' he thinks his music should appear at the moment, or who he's trying to impress."

After scrapping what had initially been prepared they spent the remaining time improvising and following Fahey's instincts. Rather than trying to control the impossible, the resulting album became appropriately entitled *The Epiphany of Glenn Jones*. A mixed bag of sound collage and some song-based collaborative material, the album retains an unhinged, unpredictable feel throughout.

After the release of these new albums, Fahey began to tour again to support himself. Back on the road, he dealt with many of the same problems. He still felt that he didn't have to impress his audience. His electric material was intentionally slow and dark, something not all Fahey fans were looking for. Fans who hadn't been keeping close tabs on his recent activities occasionally came to his shows seeking acoustic mellowness. Instead they saw an angry Fahey figuring out the nuances of electric guitar. No stranger to shrugging off criticism, he enjoyed the dissonance.

Most of his younger audience was used to such sounds and tolerated his experiments. "They have a much wider knowledge of music and noise and experimentalism," said Fahey. "I'm not dealing with hippies anymore. I always hated hippies. I ran into this chick the other night when my trio was playing here in Portland. Everybody was digging it but here comes this old chick making a lot of noise, wanting me to play shit that's forty years old. I told her 'go to hell.' She started screaming and stuff so they had to take her out. I don't care. Get lost. That stuff was too sentimental anyway."

Revisiting the technique of collage, he found that the new technology allowed him to edit and layer more efficiently than splicing tape together. Seeking the furthest reaches of out-there music, he discovered Japanese noise, a devout circle of extreme electronic musicians. "I like noise," said Fahey. "I use Merzbow [a Japanese noise artist] in my tape collages. I like the violent. It's abstract violent. When I come home exhausted and I want to lay down and forget about my obligations to other people, I'll turn on noise and enjoy it. Noise has nothing to do with people, and I don't want to think about people while I'm resting. Then I'll fall asleep, and when I wake up, I'll be ready to go and deal with people again."

He moved ever closer to the avant-garde. He began working with the Table of the Elements label, known at the time for their series of radical experimental guitar albums. Their roster included Keiji Haino, Loren Connors, and O'Rourke, among other experimentalists. It seemed ideal company. The label even attached O'Rourke to produce Fahey's next record, giving the two burgeoning friends an opportunity to collaborate on a musical level. Fahey came out to Chicago to stay with O'Rourke and his roommate Kevin Drumm, a pioneer of experimental guitar in his own right, to record the jarringly abstract *Womblife*.

In the process, Fahey abandoned guitar playing entirely. "He had these tapes and he wanted me to stack them on top of each other in various ways," remembers O'Rourke. "My studio at the time was basically a room off of the kitchen. He said he wanted to make it sound like whales rubbing the barnacles off the side of a boat. Then he would lie down on a couch in the kitchen where he could hear and I would sort of massage it together. He just said, 'Do what you need to do,' and I just sort of did electronic music-ing or whatever."

Fahey doesn't play an instrument at all on *Womblife*. Instead, he orchestrates found sounds to compose the delirious symphonies he heard in his head. "All the tracks were made with these tapes he had," recalls O'Rourke. "Kevin played on something. I played on something. I had a synthesizer at the time, but if he didn't have a tape of the sound he wanted he'd just tell us to do it."

To fend off accusations that he could no longer play the intricate fingerpicking style he was best known for, he decided to include a long solo acoustic composition, the twelve-minute album finale "Juana." The piece was intended to silence his critics, a gorgeous long-form track that recalled his Takoma heights. However, according to O'Rourke, it was not Fahey who performed it for the album. "The last track he recorded a few times, and then said he didn't want to play it anymore," recalls O'Rourke. "What happened was, the chair he was playing in had wheels on it and he leaned too hard on the front of the chair and it went out from under him. He was really big! He just said, 'I'm not playing this anymore. You play it.' So I played it.

"He wanted to put one track on there to show he could play guitar. I think one of the things about the record before was I think he was stung by people saying he couldn't play guitar anymore. He could play that track. He just didn't want to that day."

No one seemed to be able to tell the difference, and the track became an album highlight for nostalgic Fahey fans. A few years earlier, one of his prior labels, Shanachie, had suggested he rerecord his 1964 *Death Chants* album. Instead he recruited guitarist Charlie Schmidt to do a note-for-note version and passed the tapes off to the label. (He was dropped from the label before the project was released.) Uninterested in the mechanics of playing his signature fingerpicking style, he seemed all too happy to let others stand in when it suited him.

Fahey had grown stubborn in his isolation and continued to be massively difficult for those around him. On the road he seemed unable or unwilling to do basic upkeep. He brought only T-shirts and shorts for bitter winter climates. He required constant supervision from friends and concert promoters, all of whom rushed to accommodate his unpredictable needs. On tour in Boston, Coley recalls, his belt broke: "When he broke his belt he would just let his pants fall down. We were walking around Harvard Square and he was shuffling along with his pants around his ankles. I would hate to say his story is cautionary, but it's hard to say."

Some believed that he put on a show of being dysfunctional as a defense mechanism. "He had so many years of people he didn't want to deal with and idiots that he developed so many methods of deflecting," says O'Rourke. "He created a character to avoid people and then he was always that character. I think he was more in touch with reality than people give him credit for, but I just don't think it was worth his while to show that because it was a protective wall."

Jones, who had known Fahey far longer than his new 1990s experimental fans, sees it differently. "Part of that was him living up to the legend of himself," says Jones. "I saw that behavior in him when he was around younger people who were into the Fahey mythology and he would kind of play to the balcony. In the years I knew him, one-on-one he was never like that around me. I don't know how much of that was him. Certainly there was excess, stories of him eating a whole tub of ice cream. I don't think his excesses were to impress anyone. It was just his appetite. When he was a drinker he would drink to the point of obliteration and when he was a smoker he chain-smoked. When he did anything that he thought was good he would take it as far as it could go."

Fahey employed these techniques often. On the road, if situations weren't to his specifications, he found excuses to evade or sabotage things. Fahey called promoters and pretended to be a doctor, telling them that John Fahey had a heart attack. If the airport line dragged too long to catch a flight to a show, he sometimes just turned around and went home. He got creative, unafraid to make a spectacle if need be. "We were at one show and he didn't like the promoter, so he decides to pretend to go into a diabetic coma," recalls O'Rourke. "He doesn't let me in on it, I'm literally carrying him up the stairs and the promoter is behind us freaking out saying we have to call the police and John's unconscious. I'm carrying him and all of a sudden I hear this whisper in my ear: 'Keep going.' He eventually let me in on his tomfoolery, so I felt blessed even though I was a victim of it. I just don't think he could get out of the habit. He couldn't stop fucking with people. He just couldn't do it."

Coley saw Fahey's isolation with clarity. "He knew exactly what was going on, but he didn't seem to give a shit. He was impressively 'fuck you' about a lot of stuff. I assume he was a wise-ass. In his prime, especially when he was drinking, he must have been a fucking terror. The impression you got was that he was a really smart guy but had put himself perversely in this milieu where it would be impossible for him to exercise these aspects of his personality," says Coley. "It was like he was doing some weird penance. I hate to project too much onto it, but it did have a weird moral quality of self-flagellation."

Fahey's lifelong habits made him difficult to deal with, even for those who lived on the fringe of the creative worlds themselves. "I think the creative impulse was growing again. In a way it was a fight between the new impulse to do things and to him the easy life he had gotten used to, basically living hand to mouth and going to thrift stores," says O'Rourke. "It's almost like he spent so many years not giving a shit, not about being creative but just about what people thought of him. Now that he was starting to deal with people again being creative he couldn't quite get out of the habits he had for years and years. That's the way I looked at it. He was never bad to me, but he put me in situations that he didn't really want to put me into but he couldn't help it, it had been so ingrained."

Fahey enjoyed flouting conventions, pushing buttons to test people's limits. The strictures of international etiquette were to him invisible. His travels did little to restrict his behavior. "I remember we were in Germany, we were in Cologne, and he wanted to go to one of the big art bookstores, Walther König," remembers O'Rourke. "We got there and the first thing he asks for are books on Nazi propaganda.

So he buys all these books of Nazi propaganda and we go get something to eat before the show. We were sitting at the table and he starts opening these books and pointing at them and showing them to other people in the restaurant and going 'ha ha!'"

As Fahey's catalog continued to be reissued on CD, he booked bigger and bigger gigs. In 1998, Fahey was invited to perform at the Guinness Fleadh festival on Randall's Island in New York. The Irish-themed multiday event featured performances from artists like Sinead O'Connor, Van Morrison, and John Lee Hooker, among many others. Fahey used the concert as an excuse to spend a few weeks in New York. He stayed at the Hint House, a home shared by various members of the No-Neck Blues Band. As one of the city's most uncompromising group of improvisational musicians, the band often played in tunnels in Central Park and other strange locations. The group was more of a collective than a traditional band, with no set membership; Fahey thought they were a cult. He scheduled them to do some recording work for Revenant.

One of the band's more consistent members, Dave Nuss, recalls Fahey's presence as more than memorable: "Fahey stayed with [artist] Rita Ackermann and me up on the top floor of the NNCK [No-Neck Blues Band] building," he remembered. "Upon his arrival, the bathroom filled with bottles of pills on every surface. Despite the chilly temperatures, he was always barefoot and shirtless, wearing the same cutoff jean shorts, held up by a rope, for the duration of his stay. He rarely had his sunglasses off, day or night. I recall that he would play acoustic guitar sometimes, which was a joy, and he would fall asleep anywhere, anytime, for any length of time, and no sound would rouse him. We thought he was narcoleptic. I recall an incident when he was eating a banana and fell asleep holding the peeled, half-eaten banana straight into the air while his head drooped and he loudly snored."

One Hint House member felt his presence more than the rest. Sara Press lived in the house with her boyfriend at the time, Adam Mortimer. After having met her just briefly, Fahey developed an intense obsession with her. His romantic fantasies were exaggerated to unreasonable degrees. He made his affections overwhelmingly clear, however nonsensical it may have seemed. "I was living in the Hint House at the time," Press remembers. "Fahey stayed there, and I had a whirlwind experience as his muse for a few months afterwards. My Fahey name was 'Sacred Sara of the Clean Shirts.' He sent me several boxes of letters, paintings, mixtapes, and other things during that time, culminating in a marriage proposal. Just before I got the letter with the proposal and just after he mailed it, I managed to clarify my situation with him over the phone. I guess he hadn't realized I was in a live-in relationship since he mistakenly believed I lived in a cult or commune. He then became horribly embarrassed and got off the phone and never contacted me again. For my part, I thought he knew my situation all along and just didn't care. Being twenty-three at the time I didn't analyze too closely his fascination with me. I had thought it was simply a very strange friendship with someone who lived within rules of his own making."

Romantic entanglements or not, his relationship with the No-Neck Blues Band continued unabated. He even booked a US tour with the group. The chaotic nature of the young, eccentric musicians inspired Fahey. The band had no clear structures, rules, or discussions about their performances. With them, he had finally found a place where he could do anything musically, unbound by any genre or audience barriers. Fans who came to see the Fahey of the past were often startled and turned off by both NNCK and Fahey's modern, abstract takes on musicality and performance. John Fell Ryan was the most flamboyant persona in NNCK, often dressing in bell-bottoms and robes. His contributions to the group included free-associating vocal while brandishing a seven-foot shaman staff. Ryan recalls the tour receiving a mixed reception. "I was aware [Fahey's] performances were kind of bumming people out," Ryan says. "His legend was as a highly skilled and composed acoustic picker, but his style at the time was electric, detuned, slow, wandering, and always an hour too long. I didn't like the kind of fussy fan with high expectations and demands of performers, so I thought his sludgy, fuck-you delivery was appropriate. But then again, that same fussy audience had similar problems with me as a performer." Fahey enjoyed disappointing those seeking his older style.

One night during the tour, over dinner, Fahey suggested psychotherapy to the troubled young musician. Concerned, Fahey tried to impart some wisdom, seeing aspects of his own troubles in his tourmate. "His suggestion of psychoanalysis was coming from a protective understanding of going through madness himself. Later that night, Fahey came up to me again in the parking lot and told me, 'You know when you were singing "Everyone is the same"? I know what you're talking about. Everyone is the same.'

"I would claim to others that I was just riffing on Motorhead's 'Ace of Spades,' but secretly knew that Fahey knew that we both were experiencing what might be considered gnostic revelations or visions of the universe. A few days up the coast, in my hometown of Seattle, NNCK and Fahey played a set together at the Tractor Tavern. This set was striking in that Fahey put down his guitar and adopted my 'rapping' style of free verse. So we did a bit of a duet there. It was the last time I saw John Fahey alive."

RED CROSS

"Suddenly I hit desolation and just as suddenly my mother was gone, and I found myself on another kind of train headed West. And there was my wife. We were together again and headed home. Desolation was gone. You don't feel so bad when you're headed home. Desolation was gone. You don't feel so bad when you're headed towards a place that was ruined a long time ago—as when you're headed towards a good place where they are just beginning the abomination and you know it won't stop until it's all gone. I didn't want to see the process. But we were escaping, so I felt better. We could never live in Paradise, Md., but it wouldn't be there very long anyway. Nobody could stay."

—John Fahey, in his liner notes to *John Fahey Visits Washington, D.C.*, 1979

Back in Salem, Fahey once again attempted to settle down. He started dating a woman named Melissa Stephenson. She had approached him to autograph her copy of the *Anthology of American Folk Music* at a show in California, and in return he handed her a business card from the motel he was staying in. After a few visits to Salem she rented a house in nearby Kaiser, Oregon, and Fahey moved in with her.

An avid fan of his music for many decades, Stephenson was reluctantly thrilled and charmed by Fahey. The two spent time listening to albums, going out to eat, and driving around town to thrift stores, searching for records. "When John moved in he was nice, polite, eager to be a good housemate," says Stephenson. "He agreed to help with everything but never did anything. He was very entertaining, could be very funny. He told me he'd really wanted to be a stand-up comedian but was better at playing the guitar so he did that. With Fahey there's never a dull moment. He mostly liked to eat. He was somewhat ill at ease with most women, except waitresses. His interactions with men seemed normal enough. He could say a guy was a nice guy or an asshole and he was right. All women were dangerous."

The relationship quickly grew strained as he became combative. He began to come and go. Stephenson let him go, but seeing that he needed help kept an open door, offering him refuge whenever he wanted it. They lived together on and off for the next two years, during which he periodically went back to the cheap motels, until they no longer took him in due to his erratic behavior. When left to his own devices he invariably ran out of money and a hospitable place to stay.

Even though she adored him, he became impossible to take care of. "He was not in therapy while living with me, but once he was about to be evicted from the motel where he was renting a room and faked a suicide to get a free ride to Salem in an ambulance," remembers Stephenson. "They put him in the psych ward, and two weeks later, when they caught on, I got a call from Dean Blackwood asking me to take him back in because he had no place to go. They'd thrown him out of the last place that would have him. I agreed, but Dean had to convince me to some degree. And yes, John talked about having been abused by his father frequently. He'd call his father a pedophile out loud to anyone anytime he had an audience. I got tired of hearing it, and after a while I no longer believed it and asked him to stop talking about it around me."

In the summer of 2000, Glenn Jones reconnected with Fahey for the first time since the fallout from their collaborative album. Jones hoped they could work together on compiling a comprehensive set of Fahey's Fonotone material—his oldest recordings, which he cut back in Bussard's basement so many decades ago. Reluctant to revisit this music, Fahey said he would only participate for $10,000; otherwise they would have to wait until he died. Jones had learned from his prior collaborative attempts and didn't battle to persuade him. Instead, he let it go, and the two enjoyed an afternoon unburdened by expectations, hanging out and talking about records like old times. Fahey even commended Jones for sticking to his guns on their album together, while so many others would have given up in the face of such overwhelming adversity.

Fahey continued pressing forward with new music, focusing on fragments for his next album. Revenant had the Patton box set under way, and Drag City was putting together a second book of Fahey's writing, under the title *Vampire Vultures*. Although he had some assistance with his day-to-day responsibilities, he became increasingly lonely. With no partner in his life, he remained in emotional disarray. He continued to obsess over women, no matter how fleeting the interaction. His most desperate attempts at "love" were aimed toward a young Japanese woman named Hitomi. Fahey had undertaken many intensely powerful pursuits, bordering on stalking, but this was the most severe of them all. They met at a show of his in Japan, and she instantly became his all-consuming reason for being. She became a symbol of some elusive cure for his sufferings. The relationship was yet another fantasy for Fahey; his attentions were unrequited.

"I happened by Fahey, who was entering a Chinese restaurant, and he invited me along," remembers NNCK's John Fell Ryan from their time together on tour. "I wasn't hungry, but Fahey ate enough for the both of us, plus. It was then he showed me his collage book. He opened this very thick binder and leafed through it, opening page after page of cosmic New Age paintings of utopian architecture he had clipped out of books or magazines—hundreds of pages, like a phone book. Unicorns and fantasy stuff, like Roger Dean, but more down on the edge of those airbrushed galaxy paintings you sometimes see homeless men peddling on the NYC streets. There would be really weird sections, like a whole series of newspaper clippings of Tom Selleck's face. Fahey told me the collage book was a present for a woman in Japan to whom he planned on proposing marriage. He told me he had written her a letter and bought a ticket to Japan to see her."

Hitomi became the myopic center of his days and nights. He sold his possessions to Stephenson to raise money to go see her in Japan. After a barrage of marriage requests, her parents finally became aware of the situation. The obsession came to a head when he met with her family at a conference room in the Tokyo airport. Fahey tried to plead his case to them but failed. Their presence was an intervention, not a dialogue, an attempt to get Fahey to leave her alone once and for all.

"John told me the story of the confrontation," says Stephenson. "It upset him very much. You should have seen his wild eyes. I don't believe she was married, but she may have married someone after the whole John thing wound down. There were people sort of trying to rescue her from Fahey. It sounded serious to me." According to O'Rourke, the police had to get involved.

This final rejection left him despondent. He spent the cold Salem nights alone, pining for what could never be. His heartbreak became the subject of his last album released during his lifetime, 2000's

Hitomi. Much like his 1990s output, the album featured a dark stream of collaged noise and reverbed electric guitar. With titles like "Despair" and "East Meets West," the album sounded distant. Only the occasional sparse beauty of loneliness in evocation of his muse shines through an otherwise dour affair.

Like many of his albums, he recorded it himself. "While he was at home he did spend a lot of time, hours, playing the guitar using electronic noisy gadgets I cannot remember the names of," says Stephenson. "He recorded a lot of the album on cassette tapes on his boom box. Most of *Hitomi* was recorded this way in my guest bedroom. It was dark, bluesy guitar-music-slash-noise. He would get started and play the same thing over and over. Artie Shaw's 'Nightmare' was one of his favorites."

His sadness overwhelmed him and he grew even more distant. Always fascinated with religion and mortality, Fahey seems to have been prepared for death since his teenage years. The legend of Blind Joe Death, as the dawn of the new millennium approached, became less a prophecy and closer to a stark inevitability. Fahey turned sixty years old in 2000, a feat many considered incredible given his years of hard living. He had survived decades of substance abuse and mental and physical ailments, though all had taken tolls along the way. Miraculously, he seemed to triumph over his obstacles, still a forceful personality in his later years. "Those of us who knew John cannot imagine ever again meeting anyone with his iron will, his seemingly indestructible constitution and enormous appetites," Glenn Jones would write in his liner notes to Fahey's final and posthumously released album *Red Cross.* "His passions were insatiable: food, women, music, books, drugs, alcohol, cigarettes. People said Fahey never grew up, that he was a child all his life—with all that that entails, both good and bad. John's prankster charm, endless curiosity, guileless spirit, largesse, and a life lived in the present made him a delightful and engaging figure to be around. But his a-sociability, belligerence, irresponsibility and an almost constant need for gratification were exhausting."

With no one left in his life romantically, he began to recall the grace of the only woman to stand by him, and he began to regret his divorce from Melody. Since the initial shock of their split, her anger toward him had cooled. Whenever business calls for him came to the house, she got him the messages. Never fully out of contact, he attempted to bridge their friendship. Although she had remarried, her company and affection seemed his only shot for comfort. He began to feel his mortality more completely. Feeling not long for this world, he began attempting to rekindle some of his other relationships, even e-mailing Spottswood and Bussard about visiting Maryland again.

Never the picture of health, Fahey experienced more pronounced symptoms of what was soon discovered to be advanced heart disease. When he finally consulted a doctor, he was advised to undergo heart bypass surgery in an attempt to clear his clogged arteries. "He had visited a cardiologist or two in Portland who told him he was in very bad shape," says Stephenson. "He declined rather rapidly. I tried to help, but could not get a handle on what to do. I invited him out to walk the dogs and he went once. He was really not good." Decades of poor diet and little exercise had left him weak and debilitated. There were doubts from those who were still close to him as to the quality of medical care he was receiving, but with no legal or marital ties, he was left to his own in such decisions. "He was taking way too many prescription meds," says Stephenson. "Some doctors had him on fifteen to twenty different medications at once, for everything under the sun. John was a committed doctor shopper. I'd like to find those fuckers who killed John Fahey."

He scheduled an operation for a quadruple bypass at Salem Hospital, an extensive and potentially life-threatening procedure. He was advised by his doctors to get his affairs in order. Facing imminent surgery, he began to examine his life in a different, more immediate context. When thinking of the people he cared about most in the world, the first person he considered was Melody. Fahey appreciated the unconditional nature of her love for him, even after he left her. Melody, regardless of the past, came to his side to support him. "We ran into him once at a thrift store and he didn't look too good. Then I didn't hear from him for a month or two, so I phoned to see if he was OK, and he had been sick. He didn't tell me what it was. The next day he phoned and asked me and my husband, Verlyn, to come out to lunch with him. He started talking about his will. I told him he should set up a scholarship for music to UCLA. I was just joking around. Anything would go to his mother. I thought it was all a big joke. He asked about me, leaving me something, I said it was OK with me. I took it as John being melodramatic. A few days later he called and told me he was in the hospital. That was the first time I knew he had serious heart problems."

While Melody and Blackwood had high hopes for a swift recovery, Fahey calmly prepared his will—in his own unique fashion. "There was stuff to be taken care of and he was filling out forms," recalls Blackwood. "It started to get him thinking about one of the great questions of life. When faced with death, which people in your life were most deserving of something by whatever criteria you would use? He went through several versions of hand-written wills." Like his liner notes, these hazy notes would be entertaining and insightful but not confined by reasonability.

"Because his instructions were kind of crazy, Mitch Greenhill [as the executor of Fahey's estate] worked with him to make it something that could be actionable," says Blackwood. "One of the original versions had him leaving a certain amount to the Union Pacific railroad—just things that weren't really possible. It had this grand sweeping poetry as a gesture, but it made no sense as to what to do. He was infatuated with Hitomi at the time. I don't know if she was in the final version or not but it got more practical over time."

Melody became the main beneficiary of a trust formed from his estate and controlled by Mitch Greenhill and her. As the only person there for him in his final days, Fahey wanted to know that she would be provided for after he died. Maybe he still loved her too. "I just know that right before he died he wanted to move back in with me," she says.

On February 16, 2001, Fahey checked in to Salem Hospital for the operation. He seemed in relatively good spirits and appeared relaxed, even amiable. Perhaps he had accepted his fate and begun making peace with his own existence, having accomplished an engaging body of work left to be discovered for generations. Prone to anxiety throughout his life, Fahey seemed serene and calm, though a very real ordeal awaited him. "One thing I have to say is that when he was in the hospital, he treated everyone in there so gently, the nurses and the doctors and everyone, because he didn't think he was going to live," says Melody.

Melody and a few local friends were at his side as he awaited surgery. Few among them believed that it could be the end for Fahey. But the operation would be far more serious than doctors had planned. Instead of the original quadruple bypass, it became a sextuple.

"It was a lot worse than what they thought, so the operation took a lot longer, it was more complicated, there were more bypass procedures involved in the surgery itself," says Blackwood. "He did have a sense that things might not go well, even though at that point no one knew how complicated it would be when they got in there. I didn't go into the surgery thinking anything too bad was going to happen. I thought the odds were pretty good that he would recover, but he just never really regained consciousness. I wasn't physically there because I guess in my head I downplayed the chances of a negative outcome."

On February 22, 2001, after a few days on a ventilator, John Fahey was removed from life support at 9:45 AM and passed away due to complications from open-heart surgery, according to his death certificate. Those in his life were stunned and devastated by the news. "I didn't think for a second that he was going to die," said Melody. "I was totally in shock when it happened, when they told me he was brain-dead and they had to turn off the machine. I told them to wait. It was horrible. The whole thing was just horrible. But he was so sweet to everyone in there. He was very sweet to me at the end. He told me he set up this trust for me and I told him not to do it because he was going to need his money. He told me he already set it up. He knew he wasn't going to need it. He said he was happy he left this much music around for people as he had. He wasn't angry about the fact that he was sure he was going to die."

Melody had had her suspicions about the quality of his medical care, but because she wasn't his wife she felt removed from the details. Fahey himself had done little to help matters. "He was bacon-and-egging it right up to death's door," she recalls. "The night before his operation he had mashed potatoes and meat loaf. I thought it was odd. I asked the nurses if he should be eating that the night before a big operation. If I'd been married to him I would have sued them. He actually died of a bowel obstruction on the second day. They give you these paralytic drugs so you can't move. If you can't move, your bowel system can't move, and he really shouldn't have had anything in his system, but he was diabetic so that may have complicated things.

Maybe he had to eat every few hours. I don't know. It was terrible, just terrible. For a couple of years after that I would burst into tears whenever I thought about it."

Arrangements were quickly put together, mostly by Melody and her husband. Through the Internet, the word of his passing spread, and those who knew him did their best to attend his memorial in Salem. Blackwood, perhaps one of the closest associates of Fahey in his final years, had a hard time understanding how to process his death. "I didn't have a place on this spectrum of feeling except off to one end," he says. "I don't think I was bottling it up or anything, but I didn't feel that it was within my right to be devastated. I think I put off processing it for years. To be honest, I never had any big revelation moment or anything like that, which is not a testament to my stoicism but just as sort of an example of how things went down in my relationship with John. I was this dedicated trooper in his vision for an anti-sentimentalist approach to life. I was a foot soldier in that army. So to deny that at the end would have been a crime, to subvert or undermine that by getting all sloppy at the end. He had influenced me in that way."

The funeral was a closed casket affair, and John Aloysious Fahey was apparently buried in black shorts, sneakers, and an XXXL T-shirt. More than one hundred people came—friends, managers, ex-wives, musicians, and even a few Union Gospel Mission residents. Friends came to pay their respects: Glenn Jones, George Winston, Peter Lang, and Leo Kottke all made the journey. Kottke delivered a brief yet powerful eulogy crediting Fahey for launching his career and creating an avenue of expression for acoustic guitar players: "In a country full of crap, John created living, generative culture. With his guitar and his spellbound witness, he synthesized all the strains in American music and found a new happiness for all of us. With John, we have a voice only he could have given us; without him, no one will sound the same." Melody spoke as well, and a Japanese koto player Fahey admired performed.

After the service, a few musicians and friends gathered at a club to play songs and drink in his honor. Glenn Jones visited Melissa Stephenson to listen to Stanley Brothers records and go through boxes of Fahey's writings, collages, paintings, and books—the remnants of his robust creativity and the ephemera that filled his final years.

For Blackwood, the funeral was when reality finally began to set in. "That's when I started to feel the weight," Blackwood remembers. "This was it. That was the finality of it. But it was almost like I was looking around to those who were closer to Fahey in a way. I hope they weren't too devastated by this. I didn't feel in that class, even though we had spent the last decade together. Maybe that prevented me from absorbing it fully because it would be disingenuous to have a meltdown over this. It would be contrived in a way. I worked with him, but I wasn't Melody or even Spottswood, who had a long history [with him]. To that point, Kottke was really torn up and gave a nice eulogy that was great, and it was clear he was struggling with it. Maybe that reinforced what I was thinking: here was a guy who was appropriately devastated by this."

The following day there was an all-day memorial service held at a local high school. George Winston performed Fahey's "The Last Steam Engine Train" on harmonica and many friends and well-wishers came through to pay their respects. A second memorial service was held at a lecture hall at Willamette University in Salem on March 4. Although they hadn't communicated at all since 1973, his first wife, Jan, felt compelled to attend. She had read about his comeback and his tough living situation but feared interfering. She found herself the object of fascination by some of Fahey's more ardent fans and supporters, since she had been immortalized in his memoir. "I went to the memorial. As soon as they found out who I was they all wanted to touch me. I was like, 'Who are you people?' We were in a big room, and one after the other they would come up to me and tell me their story. He had to have people take care of him, and they did. It's very sad. It's really tragic. People talked about having to drive him places and people having to feed him and buy him guitars and take care of him like a giant, talented baby. They talked about what a blessing it was to have this opportunity to take care of him and I thought, better you than me. It seemed like that would have been my life if I had made different choices, but it was absolutely the right decision. Melody is a good lady. I'm sure she tried."

On February 25, the *New York Times'* Jon Pareles wrote an extensive obituary:

> John Fahey, a guitarist who carved out a private corner of Americana only to see it become a foundation of new age music, died on Thursday. . . . Playing a six-string acoustic guitar, Mr. Fahey used country-blues fingerpicking and hymn-like melodies in stately pieces with classical structures. Wordless and unhurried, his music became contemplation and an elegy, a stoic invocation of American roots, nameless musicians and ancestral memories. Behind its serene surface, the music was both stubborn and haunted.

Two years later, David Fricke of *Rolling Stone* would echo the admiration, naming him number thirty-five among the one hundred greatest guitarists of all time. Even in summation, no other musician could be credited with his achievements, his contributions rightfully seen as essential to the language of popular music:

> John Fahey created a new, enduring vocabulary for acoustic solo guitar—connecting the roots and branches of folk and blues to Indian raga and the advanced harmonies of modern composers such as Charles Ives and Béla Bartók—on an extraordinary run

of albums in the 1960s, released on his own Takoma label. Fahey knew American pioneer song in academic detail; he wrote his UCLA master's thesis on blues-man Charley Patton. Fahey was also a precise fingerpicker addicted to the mystery of the blues as well as the music, a passion reflected in apocryphal album titles such as *The Transfiguration of Blind Joe Death*, from 1965. Fahey endured illness and poverty in the 1990s, but re-emerged to a new wave of acclaim from bands such as Sonic Youth. He continued touring and recording—often on electric guitar—until his death in 2001.

EPILOGUE

I REMEMBER BLIND JOE DEATH

"I've always really thought of myself as a spiritual detective and a psychological detective. I guess with my music I'm always trying to get to a fuller understanding of myself. I felt so alienated from the culture around me, like I was from a different planet, like I wasn't really a member of the human race. I had two heads, one just wasn't visible. So I was looking for another path of music. I didn't really know what it was. I didn't care what it was and I still don't. Makes no difference to me and that's perfectly okay. 'Cause I'm just a little blip. The whole style is just a little blip on all the mainstream of music. We don't fit anywhere. And we never will."

—John Fahey, interview, 1994

John Fahey remains an ineffable presence, a touchstone. I believe this was his intention from the moment of his first recording. Seemingly, his career was in preparation for his legacy, with his copious notes and fictions providing its building blocks. His albums are the soundtracks to his story, and Blind Joe Death his alter ego. As a scholar, he saw the scope of modern music, and carved his place therein by weaving fragments of cultures and genre together in his own strange collage, bridging the storytelling immediacy of the folk tradition and the modern expanse of the avant-garde. Fahey's personality kept audiences fixated on him as much as his music.

Rather than a mishmash of ideas, his music always sounded like John Fahey, no matter what he attempted. Byron Coley explains: "There's nobody before him that has the same kind of syncretic musical qualities. He used these weird blues chords that make the melodies sound strange, in the same way that Albert Ayler was strange but familiar at the same time. He never overplays. The restraint that he shows when he was doing these incredibly strange fingerings. . . . It's a very weird self-taught quality to a lot of his conception that I just find really appealing. The DIY ethos of pressing your own record and selling it at the gas station you work at under this fake blues guys name and writing these incredibly insane liner notes. The whole package was so appealing, what was this twenty-year-old philosophy student thinking . . . What the fuck? There's no precedent for something like that."

Listeners are still drawn to Fahey for the same reasons that people like Glenn Jones were attracted to him back in 1969. The myths conjured in the texts Fahey wrote for himself and the images he proliferated created a mystery that continues to fascinate. What was he trying to tell us in all this pathology? The stories of Blind Joe Death, his experiences of Takoma Park, his loves and demons, retain potency in their presentation. His unique version of Americana, focused on the existential and the symbolism of his youth, became guideposts that grounded his wild imagination. "There was a quality to his music that I had never heard at the time," Jones recalls. "Between what he was doing with the sound and the emotional quality of his playing, it made me keep coming back to hear more. The records had a handmade quality, not a corporate look, and were hard to find at the time.

That made seeking the stuff out that much sexier in terms of just try-ing to learn more. Of course with the absurd liner notes you wanted to know more about the guy. There was this mythology that you had to weed through and try to figure out what was real and wasn't. You could only make guesses."

To many he remains a dislikeable figure. His vices and abusive-ness affected everyone close to him. And his knack for alienating those who wished to be close to him forced him into solitude. Like his music, his presence was polarizing. Some felt his lack of filters in social and professional situations cost him greater fame. Yet those same ele-ments brought the audience closer to him; he held nothing back. He admitted to his regrets and failures as freely as he acknowledged his successes. The narrative of his life, which he presented so vividly, com-bined with the haunted melodies of the music, creating a universe in which listeners could fully immerse themselves. As otherworldly as his universe might have been, they could relate to the pitfalls in his life.

Jim O'Rourke explains Fahey's ability to channel his life though his music. "John lived a bigger life than most of his listeners, and his music is an expression of that life. When people hear his music they're let into a world that is still connected to theirs but has gone farther, taken more chances, had more highs and lows than they will ever have. So it has an ecstatic quality. It's the expression of a human being who has gone through extremes in his life, but when he expresses these feelings it comes direct from the heart and is not aestheticized or turned into an abstract." This raw connection echoes the blues in its pathos but lacks its narrative and form. Instead, using similar building blocks, Fahey con-structed his own stylistic and narrative conventions, unique to himself.

"John always sounded large—not big . . . large. But it's hard for me to see John," says Kottke. "He's too close. It's like talking about my Aunt Frances. That one note floating over Bǎsho's head in Maryland

'63 or '64, long before I knew it was John, is as good as anything. It's all there in that note—an E, I'm guessing. It replicated the distance and the time, then and now. If someone really plays and really writes, it's in every note, even on a bad night. Moods and competencies come and go, and change, but the thing itself is always there, often from very early on. We usually do catch these people by accident, then we stop and turn. I miss John very much. I was walking down the street in Minneapolis a couple of years ago and passed a kid playing 'Sunflower River Blues.' That kid is John at his best."

Audiences still form an intimate connection to Fahey's music. One evening during the course of working on edits for this book, I was introduced at a bar to a woman in her early twenties. With peroxide-bleached hair and a NAPALM DEATH logo painted on the back of her black leather jacket, she gave off the affectation of nonchalance until she heard about my book about John Fahey. "I love John Fahey!" she exclaimed. I asked her why and she shrugged, saying that she liked the music. I dug deeper, reminding her that she used the word love. She didn't say she liked him or that he was cool, but her instant reaction was that she loved John Fahey. Why? As if a living example of the breadth of his reach she replied, "I don't know. His music is sad but it's not hopeless. It's complicated, I guess."

Even though he believed that ambition toward careerism was hollow, Fahey wanted to matter. That his music is continually discovered and enjoyed proves his enduring relevance. "When people ask me how good I am, I usually cop to being brilliant, even better than that, but short of genius," Fahey wrote. "But I say these things in an objective dispassionate manner because, you know, and I can't explain why, but being one of the greatest guitarists in the world simply is not very important to me. Oh, but if you took it away somehow I would be very unhappy."

SOURCE NOTES

Introduction

"Did you ever go to any of the clubs . . ." Fahey, liner notes to *Transfiguration of Blind Joe Death*, 3.

1. When the Catfish Is in Bloom

"I just watched shades of red . . ." Fahey, *How Bluegrass Music Destroyed My Life*, 53.

"I remember the night we moved . . ." Ibid., 2.

"Every day. Everywhere. And they taught me . . ." Ibid., 5.

"They made us into monsters" . . . Ibid., 17.

"Eddie glorified the neighborhood . . ." Ibid., 7.

"But it wasn't fair" . . . Ibid., 206.

"I don't know if you boys experienced . . ." Fahey, liner notes to *Voice of the Turtle*.

"They taught us to love each other . . ." Fahey, *How Bluegrass Music Destroyed My Life*, 90.

"I wanted to kill my parents . . ." Ibid., 88.

"At Mount Rainier Junior High School . . ." Ibid., 94.

"It reached out and grabbed me . . ." Ibid., 253.

"When we were still in our teens . . ." Spottswood, interview by the author.

"We had mutual friends who introduced us" . . . Ibid.

"He was subject to such mood swings . . ." Ibid.

"My first impression of John . . ." Lee, interview by the author.

"Fahey and I never hung out . . ." Ibid.

"John portrayed himself as an outcast . . ." McLean, interview by the author.

"One would have thought he was fox crazy . . ." Ibid.

"John managed to be charming . . ." Spottswood, interview by the author.

"I learned a few country-western songs . . ." Fahey, interview by Stefan Grossman.

"I don't mean to demean his talent . . ." McLean, interview by the author.

"He would give people directions . . ." Lee, "The Wolves Are Gone Now," essay in box set *Your Past Comes Back to Haunt You.*

"He was young and thin . . ." Denson, interview by the author.

"Martin's was the only thing . . ." Fahey, "The Persecutions & Resurrections of Blind Joe Death."

2. Sunflower River Blues

"Canvassing in and around Washington . . ." Fahey, "In Memory of Blind Thomas of Old Takoma."

"Where I was brought up . . ." Fahey, "Blood on the Frets," 25.

"I started to feel nauseated . . ." Ibid.

"He went from disliking it . . ." Spottswood, interview by the author.

"He would walk through the rural Southern black ghettos . . ." Lee, "The Wolves Are Gone Now," essay in box set *Your Past Comes Back to Haunt You.*

"Fahey's idea of how the South should be . . ." Lee, personal letter written summer 1961.

"Today we have a pretty good idea . . ." Spottswood, interview by the author.

"The records represented the art . . ." Ibid.

"The reason I liked Charley Patton . . ." Fahey, "Blood on the Frets," 25.

"They're coming from people . . ." Fahey, interview by Jason Gross.

"He had gotten his degree . . ." Spottswood, interview by the author.

"He had matured dramatically" . . . Lee, interview by the author.

"John was influential . . ." Ibid.

3. The Legend of Blind Joe Death

"You're not meant to feel miserable . . ." Fahey, "Blood on the Frets," 27.

"An attempt to reconstruct an old song . . ." Fahey, liner notes to *Blind Joe Death*.

"When I made my first record . . ." Fahey, interview by Stefan Grossman.

"I think he was trying to have it both ways . . ." Spottswood, interview by the author.

"The whole point was to use the word 'death'" . . . Fahey, "Blood on the Frets," 27.

"When John sent me the record . . ." Charters, interview by the author.

"I didn't think his technique was very sophisticated . . ." Spottswood, interview by the author.

"Fahey could play virtually any piece . . ." Denson, interview by the author.

"He was not chatty" . . . Ochs, interview by the author.

"My impression was that there was an old . . ." Ibid.

"I had all these pieces in my head . . ." Fahey, "Reinventing the Steel."

"There was a time when John and Ed . . ." Charters, interview by the author.

4. On the Sunny Side of the Ocean

"I remember when you'd go into a folk store . . ." Fahey, "The Persecutions & Resurrections of Blind Joe Death."

"John and I lived in one large . . ." Denson, interview by the author.

"Among these people . . ." Ibid.

"I would not say there was anything endearing . . ." Ibid.

"My relationship with John was not unpleasant . . ." Ibid.

"There is a slight chance Bukka . . ." Fahey, letter to Sam Charters, November 27, 1963.

"John recorded his second LP . . ." Fahey, liner notes to *Blind Joe Death*.

"John Fahey had made his first guitar . . ." Ibid.

"I was trying to convince the audience . . ." Fahey, "The Persecutions & Resurrections of Blind Joe Death."

"I was seeking out mean, sadistic, aggressive . . ." Fahey, *How Bluegrass Music Destroyed My Life*, 235.

"James became a frightful figure . . ." Ibid., 246.

"Although the blues field in 1964 . . ." Calt, *I'd Rather Be the Devil*, 251.

"Those rediscoveries were earth-shaking . . ." Denson, interview by the author.

"Fahey was obnoxious . . ." Weller, interview by the author.

"Bāsho was a religious mystic . . ." Charters, interview by the author.

"He was crazy" . . . Fahey, "Blood on the Frets," 28.

"Once the records began selling . . ." Denson, interview by the author.

5. Poor Boy Long Way from Home

"He said he was confused . . ." Fahey, liner notes to *Days Have Gone By*.

"I hate mellow" . . . Fahey, letter to Bill Belmont, early 1990s.

During an angry conversation . . . Lebow Fahey, interview by the author.

"One time in Venice . . ." Charters, interview by the author.

Aside from music, they had a great deal in common . . . Winters, *Blind Owl Blues*.

"I wouldn't describe him as a hard-core bigot . . ." Hansen, interview by the author.

"I was playing an Al Capp role . . ." Fahey, "The Persecutions & Resurrections of Blind Joe Death."

"I thought Fahey was rather dark . . ." Cohen, interview by the author.

"I remember one night at a show in New York . . ." Charters, interview by the author.

"He was very shy . . ." Denson, interview by the author.

Once he got a small mimeograph machine . . . Charters, interview by the author.

"I think he wanted people to listen . . ." Ibid.

"I remember he broke . . ." Hansen, interview by the author.

"futility, a hopelessness and general existential despair . . ." Undated interview, quoted in "The Great San Bernardino Birthday Party and Other Excursions," Fahey Files.

"He understood that he wasn't really good . . ." Lebow Fahey, interview by the author.

"Underneath the bravado and the outrageousness . . ." Ibid.

"Even then he always had problems sleeping . . ." Ibid.

6. Voice of the Turtle

"Turtles are my favorite animals . . ." Fahey, "Why Fahey Wants to Kill Everybody."

"I never got any input from Fahey . . ." Weller, interview by the author.

"John came in wearing a turtleneck . . ." Charters, interview by the author.

"Since 1948, after seeing the movie . . ." Fahey, liner notes to *Requia*.

"This was the frustration for him . . ." Charters, interview by the author.

"I did a rough mix of it . . ." Ibid.

"He was a prestige artist . . ." Ibid.

"Requia stinks . . ." Fahey, 1968 interview, quoted in "Requia and Other Compositions for Guitar Solo," Fahey Files.

"Vanguard needed a megahit" . . . Charters, interview by the author.

"What I have is this . . ." Fahey, *How Bluegrass Music Destroyed My Life*, 164.

"We got married here . . ." Lebow Fahey, interview by the author.

"We were young and it was fun" . . . Ibid.

"As far as commerciality . . ." Charters, interview by the author.

"He didn't say anything about the cover . . ." Weller, interview by the author.

"I'm not aware of any other musician . . ." Hansen, interview by the author.

"Notes, in those days . . ." Ibid.

"The recordings which comprise this record . . ." Fahey, liner notes to *Voice of the Turtle*.

"He was unassailably convinced . . ." Charters, interview by the author.

"With Yellow Princess, John talked about . . ." Charters, interview by the author.

"The title song was the first song . . ." Hansen, interview by the author.

"Why didn't we all? . . ." Fahey, liner notes to *The Yellow Princess*.

"That session was star-crossed . . ." Hansen, interview by the author.

"Noted icthyologist [sic] who accidentally saved . . ." Fahey, liner notes to *The Yellow Princess*.

"I did not go east" . . . Ibid.

"We started talking about the concept . . ." Bruce, interview by the author.

"John felt he was ordained to be successful . . ." Charters, interview by the author.

7. View East from the Top of the Riggs Road B&O Trestle

"When a person is that ambitious . . ." Fahey, *How Bluegrass Music Destroyed My Life*, 161.

"Christmas and Easter are the two most important . . ." Fahey, liner notes to *The New Possibility*.

"Well, the arrangements are pretty good . . ." Fahey, 1979 interview, quoted in "The New Possibility," Fahey Files.

"Robbie'd just opened for someone . . ." Kottke, interview by the author.

"John called me into the bathroom . . ." Ibid.

"I can't figure how he survived . . ." Ibid.

"John had so much contempt . . ." Charters, interview by the author.

"These beautiful, young, scantily clad women . . ." Fahey, "Blood on the Frets," 28.

"There was a famous club in London . . ." Chapman, interview by the author.

"civilized and erudite . . ." Fahey, *How Bluegrass Music Destroyed My Life*, 170.

"I felt that my intelligence . . ." Ibid., 173.

"If he had done anything like that . . ." Lebow Fahey, interview by the author.

"By the time he got home . . ." Ibid.

"Fahey and I had dinner . . ." Bruce, interview by the author.

"I didn't know what to expect . . ." Monday, interview by the author.

"I developed a mailing list . . ." Ibid.

"I had arranged to get him on a music TV show . . ." Ibid.

"Fahey hasn't made a record in two years . . ." In Fahey, "Why Fahey Wants to Kill Everybody."

"I was really crazy . . ." Ibid.

"I will remember Wilson . . ." Fahey, *How Bluegrass Music Destroyed My Life*, 100.

"Out of all the songs I ever wrote . . ." Fahey, 1972 interview, quoted in "America," Fahey Files.

"There is a pulp-mill somewhere in Maryland . . ." Fahey, liner notes to *The Yellow Princess*.

"John started feeling better about himself . . ." Lebow Fahey, interview by the author.

"After half an hour . . ." Bruce, interview by the author.

"It shocked me that John . . ." Kottke, interview by the author.

"Every day was something else . . ." Lebow Fahey, interview by the author.

"My life was going by . . ." Ibid.

8. Old Fashioned Love

"All I have ever done with music . . ." Fahey, liner notes to *The Legend of Blind Joe Death*.

"Warner's was still thinking . . ." Bruce, interview by the author.

"You had to get Fahey when . . ." Ibid.

"When John began working with Dixieland musicians . . ." Charters, interview by the author.

"I was not prepared for what I heard . . ." Hentoff, liner notes to *Of Rivers and Religion*.

"We're backstage and John is going . . ." Bruce, interview by the author.

"We were left alone . . ." Ibid.

"The show was at the Paul Masson winery . . ." Winston, interview by the author.

"John was doing everything . . ." Ibid.

"Now everyone calls him a composer" . . . Ibid.

"Few living people have had such . . ." Fahey, "Bola Sete, the Nature of Infinity and John Fahey."

"They had a service every day . . ." Fahey, "The Persecutions & Resurrections of Blind Joe Death."

"I would like to introduce you . . ." Fahey, from the pamphlet included with *Fare Forward Voyagers* (Takoma C 1035, 1973).

"John could have run it . . ." Monday, interview by the author.

"He was funny, he was smart . . ." Goldman, interview by the author.

"At the time we had this spiritual interest . . ." Ibid.

"I married John . . ." Ibid.

"Having known other musicians . . ." Ibid.

"He would always compare himself . . ." Bruce, interview by the author.

"John Fahey, who stopped by . . ." Rockwell, "John Fahey Plays Impressive Guitar at the Bottom Line."

"His guitar-playing is a deliberate . . ." Nelson, "John Fahey Is a Tough Guy."

"The folk and acoustic scene . . ." Chapman, interview by the author.

"I like to travel . . ." Goldman, interview by the author.

According to Fahey's tour manager . . . Calt, "The Illusionist."

"John was always a very funny person . . ." Brennan Fahey, interview by the author.

"John was a dynamic person . . ." Ibid.

"When I play the guitar . . ." Fahey, *The Best of John Fahey 1959–1977*, 10.

"Mastering a guitar . . ." Ibid., 13.

"What I am advocating . . ." Ibid., 12.

"So Chrysalis wanted . . ." Bruce, interview by the author.

"The reason that I got rid of . . ." Fahey, interview by Jason Gross.

"He would go on for periods . . ." Brennan Fahey, interview by the author.

"It was insane" . . . Chapman, interview by the author.

"You might pray for me . . ." Fahey, letter to Glenn Jones, 1981.

"I had a career . . ." Brennan Fahey, interview by the author.

"One year he gave $2,000 . . ." Ibid.

"If you make yourself play . . ." Fahey, *The Best of John Fahey 1959–1977*, 10.

9. Let Go

"The Void is a term" Fahey, "Finger Style Adventurer," 26.

"He hated those guys . . ." Bruce, interview by the author.

"John's main goal in life . . ." Brennan Fahey, interview by the author.

"Sometimes when you meet someone . . ." Jones, interview by the author.

"We were hanging out backstage . . ." Ibid.

"He was a very heavy drinker . . ." Ibid.

"He might have been prediabetic . . ." Brennan Fahey, interview by the author.

"For me, it was torture . . ." Ibid.

"He was about forty . . ." Robb, interview by the author.

"I would try to get him to play . . ." Ibid.

"He would mix his medications . . ." Ibid.

"I wish you knew . . ." Fahey, *How Bluegrass Music Destroyed My Life*, 207.

"He claimed he was abused . . ." Lebow Fahey, interview by the author.

"In his book he makes serious allegations . . ." Spottswood, interview by the author.

"I'm sure there was a lot of emotional abuse . . ." Brennan Fahey, interview by the author.

"John was a pretty together guy" . . . Robb, interview by the author.

"John's father was an orphan . . ." Brennan Fahey, interview by the author.

"He was showing up . . ." Robb, interview by the author.

"He got tired of it" . . . Ibid.

"I got interested in '50s rock and roll . . ." Fahey, 1990 interview, quoted in "Old Girlfriends and Other Horrible Memories," Fahey Files.

"It drove me nuts!" . . . Brennan Fahey, interview by the author.

"I don't know if I would have been that great . . ." Ibid.

"Jobs would come . . ." Ibid.

"I didn't want to have to fight . . ." Ibid.

"I didn't leave John . . ." Ibid.

10. When the Springtime Comes Again

"This new group is all for freedom . . ." Fahey, interview by Jason Gross.

"I spent a day with him . . ." Hansen, interview by the author.

"I was writing these things as an escape . . ." Fahey, "Blood on the Frets," 24.

"I didn't know when he moved . . ." Bruce, interview by the author.

"John did spend quite a bit of time . . ." Brennan Fahey, interview by the author.

"When I started hanging out with Glenn Jones . . ." Coley, interview by the author.

"People were buying the records . . ." Ibid.

"He was hilarious" . . . Ibid.

"In the current season . . ." Fahey, letter to Bill Belmont, early 1990s.

"A few record store guys . . ." Coley, interview by the author.

"I stayed in touch with him . . ." Ibid.

"I got the impression . . ." Ibid.

"All Fahey's own records . . ." Blackwood, interview by the author.

"I remember working out the math . . ." Ibid.

"When you operate in that kind of . . ." Ibid.

"He wasn't the kind of artist . . ." Ibid.

"Our initial conversations . . ." Ibid.

"They were appreciative . . ." Ibid.

"A lot of the legality . . ." Ibid.

"None of them ever got paid . . ." Ibid.

Spin named Revenant's Captain Beefheart & His Magic Band Grow Fins . . . Revenant Records, "Captain Beefheart and His Magic Band Grow Fins," Revenant Records official website.

"the Everest of all jazz boxed sets . . ." Reich, "The Music Box."

"There was a sense . . ." Blackwood, interview by the author.

11. Dance of the Inhabitants

"I'm just doing solo electric . . ." Fahey, June 2000 interview, quoted in "Georgia Stomps, Atlanta Struts & Other Contemporary Dance Favorites," Fahey Files.

"Fahey isn't an Americana thing . . ." O'Rourke, interview by the author.

"Yes, I wonder what would have happened . . ." Fahey, *How Bluegrass Music Destroyed My Life*, 146.

"He made a noose out of the sash . . ." Ibid., 205.

"He told me about the writing . . ." O'Rourke, interview by the author.

"John's life was his work" . . . Brennan Fahey, interview by the author.

"He asked me to sell them . . ." Coley, interview by the author.

"It was a place my parents took me to . . ." Fahey, undated interview, quoted in "City of Refuge," Fahey Files.

"Little of City of Refuge . . ." Jones, "Of Rivers and Revisions."

"After a Boston photo shoot . . ." Jones, liner notes to *The Epiphany of Glenn Jones*.

"Having been so closely involved . . ." Jones, "Of Rivers and Revisions."

"They have a much wider knowledge . . ." Fahey, interview by Jason Gross.

"I like noise" . . . Fahey, "Blood on the Frets," 28.

"He had these tapes . . ." O'Rourke, interview by the author.

"All the tracks were made . . ." Ibid.

"The last track he recorded . . ." Ibid.

"When he broke his belt . . ." Coley, interview by the author.

"He had so many years . . ." O'Rourke, interview by the author.

"Part of that was him living up . . ." Jones, interview by the author.

"We were at one show . . ." O'Rourke, interview by the author.

"He knew exactly what was going on . . ." Coley, interview by the author.

"I think the creative impulse . . ." O'Rourke, interview by the author.

"I remember we were in Germany . . ." Ibid.

"Fahey stayed with [artist] Rita Ackermann . . ." Nuss, interview by the author.

"I was living in the Hint House . . ." Press, interview by the author.

"I was aware [Fahey's] performances . . ." Ryan, interview by the author.

"His suggestion of psychoanalysis . . ." Ibid.

12. Red Cross

"Suddenly I hit desolation . . ." Fahey, liner notes to *John Fahey Visits Washington, D.C.*

"When John moved in . . ." Stephenson, interview by the author.

"He was not in therapy . . ." Ibid.

"I happened by Fahey . . ." Ryan, interview by the author.

"John told me the story . . ." Stephenson, interview by the author.

"While he was at home . . ." Ibid.

"Those of us who knew John . . ." Jones, liner notes to *Red Cross*.

"He had visited a cardiologist . . ." Stephenson, interview by the author.

"We ran into him once . . ." Brennan Fahey, interview by the author.

"There was stuff to be taken care of . . ." Blackwood, interview by the author.

"Because his instructions . . ." Ibid.

"I just know that right before . . ." Brennan Fahey, interview by the author.

"One thing I have to say . . ." Ibid.

"It was a lot worse . . ." Blackwood, interview by the author.

"I didn't think for a second . . ." Brennan Fahey, interview by the author.

"He was bacon-and-egging it . . ." Ibid.

"I didn't have a place . . ." Blackwood, interview by the author.

"In a country full of crap . . ." Kottke, unpublished eulogy for John Fahey.

"That's when I started to feel the weight . . ." Blackwood, interview by the author.

"I went to the memorial . . ." Lebow Fahey, interview by the author.

"John Fahey, a guitarist who carved . . ." Pareles, "John Fahey, 61, Guitarist and an Iconoclast, Is Dead."

"John Fahey created a new, enduring vocabulary . . ." Fricke, "100 Greatest Guitarists: David Fricke's Picks."

Epilogue: I Remember Blind Joe Death

"I've always really thought of myself . . ." Fahey, "The Persecutions & Resurrections of Blind Joe Death."

"There's nobody before him . . ." Coley, interview by the author.

"There was a quality to his music . . ." Jones, interview by the author.

"John lived a bigger life than most . . ." O'Rourke, interview by the author.

"John always sounded large . . ." Kottke, interview by the author.

"When people ask me . . ." Fahey, letter to Ron Cowan, November 25, 1998.

BIBLIOGRAPHY

Original Interviews

Dean Blackwood

Denny Bruce

Michael Chapman

Sam Charters

Byron Coley

Ed Denson

Jan Lebow Fahey

Melody Brennan Fahey

Deborah Goldman

Barry Hansen

Glenn Jones

Leo Kottke

Anthony Lee

Nancy McLean

Jon Monday

Dave Nuss

Max Ochs

Jim O'Rourke

Sara Press

Terry Robb

John Fell Ryan

Dick Spottswood

Melissa Stephenson

Tom Weller

George Winston

Books

Calt, Stephen. *I'd Rather Be the Devil: Skip James and the Blues*. Chicago: Chicago Review Press, 2008.

Fahey, John. *How Bluegrass Music Destroyed My Life*. Chicago: Drag City, 2000.

Fahey, John, and John Lescroart. *The Best of John Fahey 1959–1977.* New York: Guitar Player Books, 1977.

Winters, Rebecca Davis. *Blind Owl Blues: The Mysterious Life and Death of Blues Legend Alan Wilson.* Blind Owl Blues, 2007.

Articles

Calt, Stephen. "The Illusionist." Unpublished manuscript.

Fahey, John. "Bola Sete, the Nature of Infinity and John Fahey." *Guitar Player*, February 1975.

Fricke, David. "100 Greatest Guitarists: David Fricke's Picks." *Rolling Stone.* www.rollingstone.com/music/lists/100-greatest-guitarists-of-all -time-19691231/john-fahey-20101202.

Jones, Glenn. "Of Rivers and Revisions: John Fahey and Cul de Sac." Fahey Files. www.johnfahey.com/pages/revision.html.

Lee, Anthony. "The Search for Charley Patton" Unpublished manuscript, summer 1961. Personal collection of Anthony Lee.

Nelson, Paul. "John Fahey Is a Tough Guy." *Village Voice*, June 9, 1975.

Pareles, Jon. "John Fahey, 61, Guitarist and an Iconoclast, Is Dead." *New York Times*, February 25, 2001.

Reich, Howard. "The Music Box." *Chicago Tribune*, December 12, 2004.

Revenant Records. "Captain Beefheart and his Magic Band Grow Fins." Revenant Records official website. www.revenantrecords.com/musics /products/captain-beefheart-and-his-magic-band-grow-fins/.

Rockwell, John. "John Fahey Plays Impressive Guitar at the Bottom Line." *New York Times*, December 2, 1975.

Published Interviews

Fahey, John. "Blood on the Frets." Interview by Edwin Pouncey. *Wire* 174, August 1998.

———. "Finger Style Adventurer." Interview by Mark Humphrey. *Frets,* August 1980.

———. "In Memory of Blind Thomas of Old Takoma." Interview by Eddie Dean. *Washington City Paper,* September 15, 2001.

———. Interview by Jason Gross. *Perfect Sound Forever,* October 1997. www.furious.com/perfect/johnfahey.html.

———. Interview by Stefan Grossman. Stefan Grossman's Guitar Workshop. www.guitarvideos.com/interviews/john-fahey.

———. "The Persecutions & Resurrections of Blind Joe Death." Interview by Byron Coley. *Perfect Sound Forever,* May 2001. www.furious.com /perfect/fahey/fahey-byron2.html.

———. "Reinventing the Steel." Interview by Dale Miller. *Acoustic Guitar,* January/February, 1992.

———. "Why Fahey Wants to Kill Everybody." Interview by Tim Farris. *Rolling Stone,* December 24, 1970.

———. 1968 interview. Quoted in "Requia and Other Compositions for Guitar Solo." Fahey Files. www.johnfahey.com/pages/req2.html.

———. 1972 interview. Quoted in "America," Fahey Files. www .johnfahey.com/pages/am2.html.

———. 1979 interview. Quoted in "The New Possibility." Fahey Files. www.johnfahey.com/pages/np2.html.

———. 1990 interview. Quoted in "Old Girlfriends and Other Horrible Memories." Fahey Files. www.johnfahey.com/pages/girl2.html.

———. June 2000 interview. Quoted in "Georgia Stomps, Atlanta Struts & Other Contemporary Dance Favorites." Fahey Files. www .johnfahey.com/pages/georg.html.

———. Undated interview. Quoted in "City of Refuge." Fahey Files. www .johnfahey.com/pages/cr2.html.

———. Undated interview. Quoted in "The Great San Bernardino Birthday Party and Other Excursions." Fahey Files. www.johnfahey.com /pages/v42.html.

Letters

Fahey, John. Letter to Bill Belmont, early 1990s. Personal collection of Glenn Jones.

———. Letter to Glenn Jones, 1981. Personal collection of Glenn Jones.

———. Letter to Ron Cowan, November 25, 1998. www.johnfahey.com /roncowanletter.htm.

———. Letter to Sam Charters, November 27, 1963. Samuel and Ann Charters Archives of Blues and Vernacular African American Musical Culture, Archives & Special Collections at the Thomas J. Dodd Research Center, University of Connecticut Libraries.

Kottke, Leo. Unpublished eulogy for John Fahey. Personal collection of Leo Kottke.

Liner Notes

Fahey, John. Liner notes to *Blind Joe Death*. Takoma C 1002, 1964, LP.

———. Liner notes to *Days Have Gone By*. Takoma C 1014, 1967, LP.

———. Liner notes to *John Fahey Visits Washington, D.C.* Takoma TAK 7069, 1979; Chrysalis TAK 7069, 1979, LP.

———. Liner notes to *The Legend of Blind Joe Death*. Takoma TAKCD-8901-2, 1996, CD.

———. Liner notes to *The New Possibility*. Takoma C 1020, 1968, LP.

———. Liner notes to *Requia*. Vanguard. VSD-79259, 1967, LP.

———. Liner notes to *Transfiguration of Blind Joe Death*. Riverboat RB-1, 1965, LP.

———. Liner notes to *Voice of the Turtle*. Takoma C 1019, 1968, LP.

———. Liner notes to *The Yellow Princess*. Vanguard VSD-79293, 1968, LP.

———. Pamphlet included with *Fare Forward Voyagers*. Takoma C 1035, 1973, LP.

Hentoff, Nat. Liner notes to *Of Rivers and Religion* by John Fahey. Reprise. MS 2145, 1973, LP.

Jones, Glenn. Liner notes to *The Epiphany of Glenn Jones* by John Fahey and Cul de Sac. Thirsty Ear thi 57037.2 1997, CD.

———. Liner notes to *Red Cross* by John Fahey. Revenant 104, 2002, CD.

Lee, Anthony. "The Wolves Are Gone Now." Essay in box set *Your Past Comes Back to Haunt You*. Dust-to-Digital DTD-21, 2011, CD.

JOHN FAHEY
DISCOGRAPHY

Blind Joe Death
Takoma C 1002 (1959, 1964, 1967); Sonet SNTF 607 (1969)

Death Chants, Breakdowns and Military Waltzes
Takoma C 1003 (1963, 1967); Sonet SNTF 608 (1969)

Dance of Death & Other Plantation Favorites
Takoma C 1004 (1965)

The Transfiguration of Blind Joe Death
Riverboat RB-1 (1965, 1967); Transatlantic TRA 173 (1968); Takoma R 9015 (1973); Sonet SNTF 744 (1978)

The Great San Bernardino Birthday Party and Other Excursions
Takoma C 1008 (1966)

Days Have Gone By
Takoma C 1014 (1967)

The Early Sessions
Takoma C 1000 (1967)

Requia
Vanguard VSD-79259 (1967); Terra T-2 (1985)

The Voice of the Turtle
Takoma C 1019 (1968); 4 Men with Beards 4m219 (2012)

The Yellow Princess
Vanguard VSD-79293 (1968)

"March for Martin Luther King" / "Singing Bridge of Memphis, Tennessee"
Vanguard VRS 35076 (1968)

The New Possibility
Takoma C 1020 (1968); Sonet SNTF 702 (1976)

America
Takoma C 1030 (1971); Sonet SNTF 628 (1972); 4 Men with Beards 4m117 (2009)

Of Rivers and Religion
Reprise MS 2089 (1972); Edsel ED 216 (1987); Collectors Choice CCM-212-2 (2001)

After the Ball
Reprise MS 2145 (1973); Collectors Choice CCM-213-2 (2001)

Fare Forward Voyagers
Takoma C 1035 (1973); Sonet SNTF 656 (1974); Shanachie 99005 (1992)

The Essential John Fahey
Vanguard VSD 55/56 (1974)

Old Fashioned Love
Takoma C 1043 (1975); Sonet SNTF 688 (1975); Shanachie 99001 (1990); P-Vine PCD-3281 (2003)

Christmas with John Fahey, Vol. II
Takoma C 1045 (1975)

The Best of John Fahey 1959–1977
Takoma C 1058 (1977); Sonet SNTF 733 (1977); Metronome 0069.053 (1977); P-Vine PCD-3277 (2003)

John Fahey Visits Washington, D.C.
Takoma TAK 7069 (1979); Chrysalis TAK 7069 (1979)

Yes! Jesus Loves Me
Takoma TAK 7085 (1980)

Live in Tasmania
Takoma TAK 7089 (1981); Sonet SNTF 861 (1981)

Christmas Guitar Volume 1
Varrick VR-002 (1982)

The Guitar of John Fahey
Stefan Grossman Guitar Workshop (1983); Mel Bay MB95399CD (1995)

Railroad 1
Takoma TAK 7102 (1983); Shanachie 99003 (1992)

Popular Songs of Christmas & New Year's
Varrick VR-012 (1983)

Let Go
Varrick VR-008 (1984)

Rain Forests, Oceans and Other Themes
Varrick VR-019 (1985)

Christmas Guitar
Varrick CD VR 11503 (1986); Better Days CA-4196 (1989)

I Remember Blind Joe Death
Varrick VR-028 (1987); Rounder REU 1025 (1987); Demon Fiend CD 207 (1987)

God, Time and Causality
Shanachie 97006 (1989)

The John Fahey Christmas Album
Burnside BCD 0004-2 (1991); Attic ACD 1362 (1992)

Old Girlfriends and Other Horrible Memories
Varrick CD VR 031 (1992)

The New Possibility / Christmas with John Fahey, Vol. II
Rhino R2 71437 (1993); Takoma TAKCD-8912-2 (2000)

Return of the Repressed: The John Fahey Anthology
Rhino R2 71737 (1994)

"Morning" / "Evening Not Night"
Perfect 14404 (1996)

City of Refuge
Tim/Kerr 644830127-2 (1997)

The Mill Pond
Little Brother lb-009 (1997); Important IMPREC 183 (2009)

Womblife
Table of the Elements Rb37 (1997); P-Vine PCD-23014 (1999)

The Epiphany of Glenn Jones
Thirsty Ear thi 57037.2 (1997)

Things to Come (John Fahey Trio)
Wavelength (1997)

Georgia Stomps, Atlanta Struts, and Other Contemporary Dance Favorites
Table of the Elements TOE-LP-38 Sr38 (1998); P-Vine PCD-23015 (1999)

Best of the Vanguard Years
Vanguard 79532-2 (1999)

Hitomi
LivHouse 70334 90001 2 (2000); LivHouse IMPREC 030 (2003)

Good Luck (John Fahey Trio)
One Hit Records 0002 (2001)

KBOO Live (John Fahey Trio)
One Hit Records 0004 (2001)

John Fahey Trio, Vol. 1
Jazzoo Records (2002)

Red Cross
Revenant 104 (2002); P-Vine PCD-3276 (2003)

Hard Time Empty Bottle Blues
Table of the Elements Nd60 (2003)

Of Rivers and Religion & After the Ball
Warner Bros 8122-73663-2 (2003); Reprise WQCP-1167 (2011)

The Best of John Fahey Vol. 2: 1964–1983
Takoma TAKCD-8916-2 (2004); P-Vine PCD-3300 (2008)

The Great Santa Barbara Oil Slick
Water 139 (2004)

Americana Masters, Volume One
Digital Masterworks International (2004)

Americana Masters, Volume Two
Digital Masterworks International (2004)

Americana Masters, Volume Three
Digital Masterworks International (2004)

Sea Changes and Coelacanths
Table of Elements TOE-85 (2006)

Addendum
Vanguard 942-2 (2006)

Vanguard Visionaries
Vanguard 73160-2 (2007)

Twilight on Prince Georges Avenue
Rounder 11661-9093-2 (2009)

Your Past Comes Back to Haunt You
Dust-to-Digital DTD-21 (2011)

The Transcendental Waterfall: Guitar Excursions 1962–1967
4 Men with Beards 4m600 (2012)
(Contains *Blind Joe Death* 4m201, *Death Chants* 4m202, *Dance of Death* 4m203, *Great San Bernardino Birthday Party* 4m204, *Transfiguration of Blind Joe Death* 4m205, *Days Have Gone By* 4m206)

INDEX